BREAD
&
OIL

Majorcan culture's last stand

Tomás Graves

GRUB STREET · LONDON

For Carmen

Oli de m'ànima, pa de mon cor
mare de ma Žlla i amor, tot amor.

This edition published in 2006 by Grub Street,
4 Rainham Close, London SW11 6SS
email:food@grubstreet.co.uk
web: www.grubstreet.co.uk

Reprinted 2006

First published in Spain *as Volem pa amb oli* in 1998
The original Catalan text © Tomás Graves, 1998
The English translation © Tomás Graves, 2000, 2006
Copyright this UK edition © Grub Street 2006

Line drawings in the text are by Laetitia Bermejo.

**A catalogue entry for this book is available from the
British Library.**

ISBN 1 904943 52 7

Typeset in Bembo, 12 on 14 point

Printed in India

Contents

pa amb oli: *a dish very frequently consumed by families of modest means, consisting of a slice of bread soaked in oil and sprinkled with a little salt or sugar.*

(Alcover's Catalan–Valencian–Balearic Dictionary)

Acknowledgements

All my Majorcan informants have been thanked in the original Catalan edition; I can only add my gratitude to Beryl Graves and Frank Riess for their invaluable comments on my translation, and to Piers Russell-Cobb for finding someone willing to publish a treatise on bread & oil outside its natural habitat. Thanks also to my Spanish publisher, José J. de Olañeta, for his support and collaboration, and again to all the artists involved.

The intuitive reader may realize how much I enjoyed writing this book, but he will never know how many new friendships were struck up in the course of researching it.

Preface to the English edition

The language of bread & oil

Much as I dislike its connotations, Majorca is the correct English name for the Mediterranean island on which I was born and have made my home. It is also closer to the original Latin *Maiorca* than the Spanish and Catalan name, *Mallorca*. In one generation, the island has undergone one of the most radical cultural and geographical changes of any region in Europe. From a sleepy agricultural society in the Francoist nineteen-fifties, still subject to a provincial aristocracy and with a very small middle class, it jumped into the service industry in the sixties, and over the next two decades the face of the island changed beyond recognition. A rural Majorcan of my age lived the kind of childhood that your great-grandparent might remember.

I wrote this book in Catalan, to which Majorcan bears the same relation as Glaswegian or Jamaican does to English: yes, it's the same language and no, it isn't. When a Majorcan villager asks for directions in Barcelona, he receives the same blank stares as a Rangers supporter or a Brixton Rastafarian might when approaching a resident of Belgravia. Occidental Catalan is spoken on the eastern seaboard of Spain from Alicanteas as far as Lleida, while

Oriental Catalan is spoken from Tarragona to Perpignan and as far east as the Balearics and the Algher area of Sardinia. Dialects then include Valencian, Catalan of the Principality, Rosellonese, Algherese, Majorcan, Minorcan and Ibizan, etc. The Barcelona dialect is considered linguistically the poorest, yet is the most widely divulged.

The Catalan language, along with Basque and Galician, was seen by Franco's regime as a threat to national unity, and their use was forbidden in public until the 1960s. Although as a literary and spoken language it is as old as Spanish, Catalan wasn't allowed to be taught in public schools until the 1980s, except for a brief period before the Civil War, during the Second Republic. Today it is again the basis of social relations and shares with Spanish the status of co-official language in all those Catalan regions with auto-nomous governments (Valencia, Catalonia and the Balearics), yet only those under thirty and a minority of the over-seventies can read and write it correctly. This reduces the potential readership of a Catalan book in Majorca to a few thousand; half the population is made up of mainland immigrants and foreign residents. Many middle-class Majorcans of my age grew up with their backs to their own language and culture. Now they are having to take Catalan classes—known as 'recycling'—if they want to enter politics or get a job in education, the civil service or even a savings bank.

So why didn't I write directly in plain Spanish, which all the islanders understand? Simply because the subject matter itself, a candid social portrait of our island disguised as a food book, insisted that it be written in the local language. Since one is obliged to write in 'official' Catalan which is rather bland compared to the 'salty' Majorcan dialect, I chose to get around the problem by quoting a lot of my informants verbatim, in italics, to preserve the flavour of the spoken language. In the present edition, italics are reserved for foreign words, so all my quotes will be in quotes.

The Catalan and Majorcan literary scene has been slow in growing from the bottom up; it has concentrated rather self-consciously on bringing an eight-century-old tradition up to date, instead of actually saying much of interest. The only area where it has caught the popular imagination is in rock and rap lyrics, graffiti and fanzines, offshoots of the protest songs of the seventies. New voices are emerging, spurred on by literary prizes, but *Volem Pa amb Oli* is more in line with the rock lyricists than with any serious writers. Many Majorcans have told me that it was the first book they had been able to read in their own language without reaching for the dictionary; that's thanks to my limited Catalan literary vocabulary, which permits no showing off. The title, literally 'We Want Bread and Oil', comes from a popular ditty akin to 'Give us some figgy pudding' but with nationalist connotations. It was in fact sung by Majorcan political prisoners while on hunger strike against conditions in Franco's jails and, more recently, by anarchist groups and conscientious objectors on street marches.

The Balearic market for our own culture is so limited compared with the six million Catalan consumers on the mainland, that most of it has to be subsidized, creating a very boring cultural panorama. New guides to the local cuisine, architecture, history, geography, art and literature appear weekly, sponsored by savings banks, newspapers and institutions, but very little emerges from the grass roots except for fringe theatre, radical groups' manifestos or fanzines. Majorcan cookery books abound, but as restaurants try out fancy versions of traditional dishes on new up-market visitors (mainly German) which have replaced the holiday-makers (mainly British), so local publishers go for coffee-table glossies in which the photographs outweigh the recipes, and whose profits come from foreign-language editions. I thought it was time to defend the true essence of Majorcan—and Mediterranean—food, which is basically cheap and cheerful: whatever is in the larder or in the kitchen garden.

English readers, especially buyers of Grub Street books, are probably better informed about Mediterranean food and culture than the Mediterraneans themselves, so I apologize if I cover some familiar ground which the Majorcan reader hasn't had access to. The channel followed today by both culinary literature and food distribution is from the productive south to the consuming north. Since the demise of sea trade, there is little cultural interchange between Mediterranean cultures; like the air routes, the axis is vertical. It is much easier to find Greek or Turkish food in London or Hamburg than in Madrid or Morocco. Such typical Mediterranean products as hummus, black olive paste or *tahini*, all available in any British high-street supermarket, are virtually unknown in Spain, as probably common Spanish products—chufa, chorizo or *turrón*— would be in Greece or Italy.

This is a direct translation of the original Catalan text and I've added an afterword to this second British edition as well as updating some of the information in the 'Oily Pages'.

I assume the reader to be passingly familiar with Majorca, although much of the information is applicable to any Mediterranean island. All but three of the illustrations were commissioned for this book, for which the artists—all Majorcans or permanent residents on the island—were paid in bottles of virgin olive oil.

Tomás Graves
Deià, 2006

TRADITIONS

Chapter 1

Whetting the appetite

Habits evolve into customs, customs into institutions, institutions into whole cultures. Habits are personal ('a Briton has the habit of taking his tea every day at five o'clock'), customs are shared habits ('the British have the custom of taking tea at five'), institutions are customs which are socially recognized and fixed ('the institution of the five o'clock tea is still alive in Britain') and a culture is all that which surrounds a custom ('tea-cakes and biscuits form part of the British tea culture'). The same goes for the beer in Germany, football in Brazil, the siesta in Andalucia or bread & oil—*pa amb oli*—in the Balearic Islands. To eat bread and olive oil is a daily habit of most of the inhabitants of the archipelago, where it is already a millennial custom; a *pa amb oli* supper is an institution in many households, and there is also a true bread & oil culture, upon which this book intends to reflect. Sadly, the term '*sa cultura d'es pa amb oli*' has recently taken on the negative connotations of narrow-minded provincialism. For example, if the local government should reject your proposal for a hundred-million-euro project, a Museum of Virtual Art at Sa Faixina, you'd probably yell: 'Shortsighted philistines! Anyone would think we're in the Third World! That's *sa cultura d'es pa amb oli* for you!'

The time has come to vindicate and exalt this bread & oil culture in its truest sense, because it sums up the best of our insular and Mediterranean selves. On the one hand, it reflects a simplicity, frugality, honesty and respect for tradition while on the other, the capacity to open up and adapt to outside influences without losing one's own identity. Partaking of a *pa amb oli* can be a solitary ritual conducive to introspection and withdrawal; but, if shared, it can lead beyond participation, into conversation and even end up as a party. Sharing a snack or supper of bread & oil calls for a bit of a chat; within the fabric of this book I've woven some coloured threads which are the words of those who can express themselves better than I possibly could in '*sa nostra lengo*', Catalan as it is spoken in the Balearic islands. I must admit that I began to write this book in standard Castilian Spanish, thinking of access to a wider readership, yet the spirit of *pa amb oli* wouldn't allow me to follow that trunk road but instead diverted me along the cobbled alley of our own language, which is more familiar but also more likely to trip me up.

I have no Majorcan blood or surnames[1] and if I consider myself a local lad it's not so much for having been born in Guillem Massot street in Palma or attending the village school, as for having suckled from the same breast as the majority of islanders: the *setrill*, the olive oil cruet. If children who share the same wet-nurse are known as 'brothers in milk', then consider me your 'brother in oil'.

At the age of four, I came down with measles. The first sign of recovery, after a few days in bed, was this plea:

---

[1] In Spain, one inherits both parents' surnames, the father's first, although a new law allows one to invert the order.

'Mother, I want a *pa amb oli*.' At home, we have always taken the question of olive oil fairly seriously. We have more than fifty olive trees, and any casual visitor who drops by the house between October and February is likely to be handed an olive-picking basket. One year, a group of US students spent a winter in our village on a creative writing course, and my father would lecture them while they picked olives for him.

While I was studying typographic design at the London College of Printing, on one of those cold February days when not even a squirrel can be seen in Battersea Park, I came down with a case of that home-sickness which all of us who have been born on *sa roqueta*[2] have felt at some time or another, so I decided to perk myself up with a good plate of bread & oil. No sooner said than done: I popped into the local Sainsbury's to buy bread (sliced), tomatoes (from a greenhouse) and olive oil (with as much colour and character as sewing-machine oil). The insipid, colourless result was no more than a plastic parody of the original. The Watts family, who rented me a room and who had heard me rabbit on about Mediterranean food, stared open-mouthed: 'You mean you Majorcans eat THAT?'

It immediately dawned on me that a *pa amb oli*, like experience itself, is not transferable. That is to say, as a concept, it doesn't 'travel well', because its identity depends totally upon having the authentic ingredients at hand, and there's no two ways about it.

Appellation contrôlée

We've all seen it written in any manner of ways: pamboli, p'amboli, pambolli, pa'amb oli, Pan Boli. I've heard that a

---

[2] 'The little rock' (in the middle of the sea).

cafeteria in Madrid displays a neon sign announcing PAN AND BOLY.

Pa amb oli is a generic term; one has to distinguish between *pa* (bread) and *un pa* (a loaf). To be correct, we cannot speak of a *pa amb oli* (unless we're talking about lubricating the whole loaf) nor of two *pa amb olis*; nor, if we want to split hairs, of two *pans amb oli*; the correct form would be two plates (or rations) of *pa amb oli*. Having cleared up this point, I can now say that, quite frankly, I'm not going to be finicky and I shall continue to say '*un pa amb oli, dos pa amb olis…*' like any other Majorcan.

The term *pa amb oli* means exactly that: bread and olive oil. It usually includes salt and scrubbed garlic, or sugar instead of salt for kids, if the oil is too strong or rancid. For the majority of today's islanders, the term includes tomato (in slices or scrubbed onto the bread) but most of the older generation still make a distinction: 'In Catalonia, they always say *pa amb tomàquet*, they don't mention the oil. We Majorcans, on the other hand, distinguish between *pa amb oli i tomàtiga* and just plain *pa amb oli*. When I was a child, I'd ask my mother for a slice of *pa amb oli*, and she would give it me plain. If I wanted it with tomato, I'd have to ask for it specially.' The tomato, like the potato, is of course a relative newcomer—a question of centuries, not millennia—and neither has yet been granted full citizenship.

Rich food, poor food

According to Madò Antònia of Ca n'Amer in Inca, for all the poverty our island has endured, 'there has never been such a thing as *cuina pobra* in Majorca, only the occasional cook poor in spirit.'

The Majorcan *haute cuisine* or *cuina de senyor*, served at the tables of the landed gentry, has received a big push lately at the expense of the authentic peasant fare, because today we're all *senyors*, more interested in satisfying our curiosity and palate than our body and soul. To find your roots, you have to get your hands and knees dirty; the rest is trunk and foliage. There are plenty of books on sale with full-page, four-colour glossies of Majorcan dishes, each more *recherché*, sophisticated and aesthetically presented than the last, none of which was ever tasted by 99 per cent of the population. Yet the reader will be lucky to find four lines dedicated to the basis of the diet, bread & oil. Shouldn't we be ashamed of ourselves?[3] People say to me, incredulously: 'You mean to say you're writing A Whole Book about bread and oil?', as if the subject warranted no more than a paragraph. Oh, come on! People write doctoral theses on germs you can't even see without your reading glasses, so why is there no book written about this age-old invention? For centuries it was the pillar of the Balearic survival diet. It was the only thing left between hunger and starvation, feeding generation upon generation of islanders, and without it many would not be here today: it deserves full recognition. Perhaps this dish has been edited out of the cookery books because it appears too simple and thus unworthy of occupying space reserved for fancier recipes. The way I see it, preparing a plate of bread & oil is like playing good rock 'n roll; it's so simple that few people can do it properly. The perfect *pa amb oli* has two

---

[3] In Majorcan and Catalan, the number four is an all purpose measurement denoting scarcity; *no ha plogut més que quatre gotes*, no more than four raindrops fell, i.e. there was hardly a drop of rain; in Minorca, *hi havia quatre jais i un boi*, there were only four old codgers and a boy, i.e. hardly anybody came.

Forty is another popular number and is used (probably because of its biblical connotations of Jesus's forty days in the wilderness, the forty days of Lent) in all sorts of blasphemous expressions. 'Forty cartloads of scalded whores!' I overhead an old lady exclaim as she tripped on the mule steps.

secret ingredients: honesty and appetite, neither of which are easy to find in the Balearics since we've become a society of abundance, indifference and cynicism, treating our islands as a tourist destination rather than the place in which we live.

The bread & oil Mediterranean tour

Greece, late autumn 1971. Three hippies—myself and two friends who (supposedly) studied at the CIDE in Son Rapinya—having made and sold leather belts during the summer and bought a beat-up VW bus in Paris with the proceeds, have finally made it, after many adventures, to the end of the road: the bottom of the Peloponnese peninsula. Fifty miles of winding dirt roads over the mountains, have brought us, famished, to the ancient walled city of Monemvassia, at the foot of a great peninsular outcrop of rock which reminds us of Alaró castle but set in the sea. No cars are allowed in the town, so we walk over a causeway and through a gate in the wall. Silence; it's Sunday, off-season, everything is closed. Finally we find a place that will serve us some fried sardines, a loaf of *khoriatico* bread cut into thick slices, with very strong olive oil, sea salt and fresh oregano. This bread and oil makes us feel at home, but we all agree that the *retsina* isn't a patch on our local Binissalem wine, and in fact tastes like Harpic.

North Catalonia (South of France), 1979. During the ten years that Salvador López and I accompanied the Majorcan singer-songwriter Toni Morlà—who nick-named our trio *Fam, Fam i Gana* (Hunger, Hunger and Appetite)—we represented the Balearic Islands at many music festivals throughout the Catalan-speaking Mediterranean. In the Roussillon area we performed at the Catalan Summer

University in Prada and at a theatre in Perpignan, once a colony of the Kings of Majorca. The billboards were plastered with posters announcing a musical show called *Pa Amb Oli*, but it seems that the dish goes by a different name in that part of Provence. Between Toulon and Nice especially they call it *pain bagna*, which I'd describe as a cross between our *pa amb oli* and Italian garlic bread. Traditionally, *pain bagna* was made with a soft, round roll, fairly flat like Moroccan bread; today it's usually made with a French loaf or a *baguette*. The bread is sliced in half horizontally, the two halves scrubbed with a juicy tomato, sprinkled with salt and irrigated generously with olive oil before being closed again. A few more drops of oil anoint the outside, the whole is placed in a hot oven for a few minutes (today wrapped in tin foil so it doesn't dry out) and it is eaten warm: crisp on the outside, soft and juicy on the inside.

Tangiers, March 1986. The ferry from Algeciras has arrived several hours late, well after midnight, but that makes no difference to our friends Ralph and Mitsuko who keep an eye on maritime traffic from their pensión terrace overlooking the port. As the ship pulls in, they saunter down to the docks and are waiting to welcome Carmen and me on the far side of the passport control. Hugs and kisses, and then the serious question:

'Where can we get a bite to eat? We're starving!'

'Nothing's open at this time of night except for the kebab stalls in the Gran Zoco.'

Having unloaded our gear at the Pensión Marrakech, we stroll through the narrow, silent streets to the enormous square where one or two minuscule market stalls, no bigger than a Majorcan larder, are still open. There's just one table, affording a tight fit for the four of us. The stallkeeper, wearing a chelabha, is toasting bread on a charcoal brazier. He greets Ralph effusively, although the name comes out as 'Brow'. We all converse in Spanish, which is still spoken by many Tangerines.

'Welcome, I like night people,' he says as he turns the bread over the coals. 'This is best food ever invented: toasted bread with oil, a bit of salt and garlic.'

We're in another world, but this makes us feel at home. No wine, however, but a glass of sweet green tea, with a sprig of fresh mint.

Wherever you tie up your boat or hitch up your donkey in the Mediterranean, you're sure to find bread and oil in some form or another. In the Rif mountains, an afternoon visitor will be received with a bowl of oil and bread to dip in it. In Tunisia, the bread is soft with a very fine crust, almost a *brioche*, and is eaten with olive oil and *harissa* (a paste hot enough to cauterize your palate) accompanied by some local olives, a variety much smaller than ours. Even the children take bread, oil and *harissa* sandwiches to school.

In the Lebanese mountains the bread is unleavened, soft and thin like a pancake. The local version of bread & oil is to pour *zaatar* onto it, roll it up and eat it, accompanied by olives and yoghurt. The *zaatar* mixture (olive oil, ground sesame seeds and oregano, though every household has its own recipe) is also poured onto a cake known as *manuxi* before it is popped in the clay oven.

Bruschetta is eaten throughout the Italian peninsula, although it varies in form and name according to the region; in Florence, for instance, it is known as *fetunta*, from *feta* (slice) and *unta* (fat or oil). *Bruschetta* is usually made from a round white loaf, a salted version of our *pa mallorquí*. The slices are toasted, scrubbed with garlic and doused in oil. Salt and ground black pepper are sprinkled over the *bruschetta*, which can also be eaten with tomato—scrubbed or diced—and dusted with oregano. It is served with slices of raw mushrooms, a bit of Parmesan cheese or slices of *capocolo*, a white pork sausage, and, of course, a robust red wine. The *bruschetta* has begun to conquer the world, in the wake of *pizza*, *pasta* and Italian ice-cream. You have to hand it to the Italians: they have a genius for self-promotion and know how to sell their products and culture like nobody else. They even know how to sell what isn't theirs as if it were: fifty per cent of the Spanish national production of olive oil—a quarter of the European total—is bought wholesale by Italian intermediaries, bottled and sold as Italian produce!

Of all the countries bathed by the Mediterranean sea, only Egypt lacks a bread-and-oil culture; there, the most common fat (as in many ex-British colonies) is clarified butter or *ghee*. Today, the olive is considered a good bet for the future and plantations begin to appear in the semi-arid edges of the desert, but in a cultural void as it were: the only traditional oil presses are to be found in Coptic monasteries, where the olive oil habit still survives from ancient times. Yet an olive tree is as foreign to the average Egyptian as a sesame plant or pistachio tree might be to us Majorcans, although all have been cultivated in the Mediterranean basin since Biblical times.

About half of all European olive oil comes from Spain, followed by Italy, Greece, Portugal and, a long way behind, France. On the Spanish mainland, although the olive tree is fairly widely distributed, the bread-oil combination can be found wherever the locals speak with an Andalusian or Catalan accent. This forms a crescent whose outside edge follows the Mediterranean coast in a southwesterly sweep

from France to Gibraltar, then to the Atlantic flatlands of
the Portuguese border. Anywhere outside this arc, bread is
usually eaten dry, or, at most, dipped in wine. A *bocadillo de
queso* in the Castilian heartland consists of two things:
bread, cheese, and you can stop counting. From La Mancha
northwards and eastwards, the people are noble and
generous but not the type to attach frills; order lamb in a
Segovian restaurant and you will get a quarter of the
animal on your plate, but don't expect a single potato chip
or lettuce leaf.

Following the olive oil crescent, the groves produce
more oil (although not necessarily better) as we head south
from Gerona and then west towards Jaen, skipping out
Murcia and Almeria. To be able to compete with the
productive Andalucians, the Catalan growers have to
concentrate on quality, opting for organic farming
techniques and the *appellation contrôlée*; a litre of organic
extra virgin oil, cold-pressed from *arbequina* olives and
bottled with all the right stamps, will bring in five times as
much as a litre of oil sold to an Italian intermediary for
refining. Andalucia of course produces some oils of
outstanding quality and has its own *appellations contrôlées*
such as the oils of Baena, but by and large their olive
industry depends upon mass production. An Andalusian
peasant considers his bread to be simply a sponge for his
oil. I've seen a Cordoban peasant take a half-kilo loaf, slice
off one end, pull the crumb out by burrowing with his
fingers, fill the crust (as if it were a canteen) with olive oil,
pouring the excess back into the oil jar. He will then stuff
the crumb back inside, squeeze the loaf a couple of times
and share it with his fellow olive-pickers. This, on a smaller
scale (a roll, not a loaf) is known as the 'Andalusian
Breakfast' and has lately been the subject of an institutional

campaign, promoted by the autonomous government, as a healthy alternative to taking junk food to school.

In Catalonia, on the other hand, bread & oil became bread & tomato (*pa amb tomàquet*, commonly known as *pantumaca*) almost as soon as the tomato began to percolate down from high-society kitchens. The general tendency has been towards more tomato—even rubbing it on both sides of the slice—and less oil. Thanks to the Barcelona-Madrid air-shuttle, the *Madrileños* now know what a *pantumaca* is, although they interpret it in their own way. In a fun-fair in El Escorial, just outside the capital, I saw *Pantumaca Auténtico* advertised in one of those Mexican-cantina-style eateries which seem to be the gastronomic equivalent of the ghost-train. After so many days of dry bread and *chorizo*, my mouth began to water. I was handed two slices of dry bread on a plastic plate, each smeared with cold canned tomato purée. This is about as far as you can get from the original without being taken to court on a charge of libel, although I suppose even a frankfurterless hot-dog daubed with ketchup could get away with the name *pantumaca* on a technicality. I shudder to think what could be served up in the name of *pa amb oli*: Scandabrod dipped in Castrol GTX?

Migrant bread & oil

The Balearic Islands, especially Majorca, has been a land of emigration during the first half of the twentieth century (extreme poverty) and immigration during the second half (tourism). Most of the immigrants who arrived to service the tourist boom—waiters, bricklayers, bus drivers —came from the poorer parts of Spain, including the olive-growing areas in the south. In their new home they could keep to their traditional diet because both the climate and the local produce were similar. In spite of differences in language and social customs, the process of adaptation of the *peninsulars* was lubricated by a shared culture of bread & oil.

The second wave of settlers came from the north: people looking not so much for work as for a better and cheaper way of life. These new immigrants had nothing in common with the Mediterranean diet or climate. There were two alternatives open to them. The easiest, for those who were only escaping the cold, was to turn their sun-tanned backs to the local culture and create jingoistic coastal ghettos, with the self-sufficiency of a Little Italy or Chinatown. Those who were looking for something more took the alternative of 'going native' and settled down in the hinterland, adapting to the local lifestyle (or what was left of it) in the measure that body and spirit could acclimatize. This rockier path was cleared in the fifties by the *barbuts* (bearded beatniks in espadrilles or sandals), beaten into a track by the long-haired barefoot *jipis* in the sixties, and recently asphalted by young executives in black convertible Mercedes and white four-wheel-drive Vitaras. Many of these modern Visigoths, Saxons and Vikings have discovered that the secret of bread, oil and red wine allows them to rock comfortably in the cradle of civilization, and to unveil the mysteries of the Mediterranean essence.

The immigrant not only receives communion with this divine essence whenever he prepares a *pa amb oli*, but also officiates in a symbolic interracial marriage every time he combines it with elements from his own mother culture, be it *chorizo* sausage, sauerkraut, rollmop herrings, Roquefort cheese or even Branston Pickle. In the New World, the African slaves conferred the powers of their outlawed animist gods upon the respectable Catholic saints; here, the local-born children of foreign parents can similarly get away with eating 'weird foreign stuff' as long as it accompanies a *pa amb oli*. This mixed marriage through bread & oil, this cross-breeding to which I confess I belong, points towards the multi-cultural future of the human race.

Children's bread & oil

If *pa amb oli* has a special place in the heart of every Majorcan, it is thanks to the sense of pride and independence we each felt when we were able to make one all by our little selves. There are many fully grown adults who have no idea how to fry an egg, but you'd be hard put to find a Majorcan above the age of reason who couldn't make an exquisite *pa amb oli* easier than falling off a donkey. 'I think that bread & oil is so easy to prepare that a mother can involve her toddlers in the process. If they're too young to cut the bread, at least they can enjoy dribbling on the oil and rubbing the tomato. And instead of using bread, they can always use an Inca biscuit[4] which can be split open with a tap on the edge of the table.'

In fact, in the old days before play-schools, the children of working mothers in the villages were looked after often by a lady known as *Sa Mestra d'es pa amb oli*, the Bread & Oil Mistress, because she would hand out a roll with oil and sugar for elevenses. My old friend Toni Viler remembers that when he was a toddler, the *Mestra d'es pa amb oli* in Andratx 'wasn't just wrinkled, she was full of chasms!'

---

[4] See page 75.

Glossing your bread & oil

I asked Toni, a born *glosador*, whether he had written any *glosa*[5] on the subject of bread & oil. 'No,' he answered, 'but I'll improvise one right now for your book…' Here it is, translated literally:

This was, and it still is[6]

If only it weren't for the 'if onlies'
The way things are is the way they'd be;
One and one would be two
Two and one would be three.

Oil and olives from the olive tree,
bread and flour from the wheat
is what the Majorcan, when in love, will eat;
and the more he eats, the more his mouth waters.
He'll find all manner of combinations
with which to make it a full meal
and the better to enjoy it; then it's *bon voyage*
to his bread & oil in good company.

Bread and oil, a pinch of salt,
tomato, sliced or rubbed upon it,
perhaps some flakes of herring,
a couple of tender caper buds,
a light green pepper, the bread well toasted

---

[5] A *glosa* is a popular local improvised verse form, the word having the same roots as our 'gloss' (comment) and 'glossary'. Often matches are staged between *glosadors*, each having to pick up the rhyme from his opponent and try to outwit him in verse. They are mostly very bawdy rhymes in a *a-b-b-a* structure, but some more sophisticated ten-line forms lend themselves to deeper philosophical comments on local life.

[6] Majorcan fairy stories begin with '*Això era, i no era…*' ('This was, and it wasn't…')

and scrubbed with spring-garlic.
Bread & oil with milk or cocoa
to keep you morning company;
maybe a shot from the *porró*[7] of wine,
and some cheese to round it off.

Clarity, health and happiness:
to improve upon our daily bread
the only way would be to pray
that we be given, can't you guess,
our daily bread & oil instead.

---

[7] A pear-shaped wine carafe with a long spout, designed for drinking in company because it doesn't touch anybody's lips; the jet of wine is directed at the back of the throat.

Chapter 2

Rudiments of Bread & Oil

I've found a couple of *pa amb oli* recipes in cookbooks published in mainland Spain; the first in Barcelona, the second in Madrid. Let's take a look:

'Majorcan *Pa Amb Oli*
Slices of farmhouse bread, sliced tomato dressed with olive oil
This is how the Majorcans denominate *pa amb tomàquet*. It is usually eaten accompanied by some black or split green olives, or, in the evenings, with an omelette.'

'*Pamboli* (Balearic Islands)
Quantities per person: 2 slices of brown farmhouse bread, virgin olive oil, two thin slices of cured ham, one ripe tomato, black olives.
Toast the bread lightly, rub it with the split tomato, place the ham between the slices and eat it accompanied with black olives.'

I doubt if many Balearic islanders would recognize their daily bread & oil in either of these sketchy definitions of *pa amb oli*, just as I imagine that few French or Italians would agree with my portrayal of a typical *pain bagna* or *bruschetta* in the last chapter. There are as many techniques as people in the Balearic archipelago, and the problem of reaching a holistic view of the definitive *pa amb oli* reminds me of the Sufi story of the blind sages trying to agree upon the definition of an elephant, each having touched a part of the body.

'It's like a great undulating serpent....'

'No, it's like a great cabbage leaf....'

'You're both wrong, it's like a mighty pillar....'

A few years ago, a group of Majorcan kids were invited along to a nationally televised children's programme and at one point were asked to make the 'typical Majorcan bread & oil'. They were each provided with the same ingredients, but only one child applied them to the bread in the 'correct' order: tomato, salt, olive oil. Forty cartloads of sacred whores! There *is* no correct order! Every child there should have won a prize. The order in which the ingredients are applied to the bread depends upon geographic factors (whether you are born in the mountains, on the plain or the coast), upon family traditions, personal taste, and even upon the quality of the ingredients (whether the bread is soft or raspy, toasted or not, whether the tomato is sliced or scrubbed). For example, the lead guitarist with the Pa Amb Oli Band, a Welshman married to a Majorcan girl, soon noticed that his father-in-law's family (olive-growers from the mountains) always poured the oil on first, whilst his mother-in-law's family (from the tomato-growing town of María de la Salut on the plain) would always scrub the tomato on first. I recently gave a talk on the subject of Bread and Oil to inaugurate Majorcan Cookery Week in Campos, and asked those present—about fifty housewives—to raise their hands if they put the oil on first. Only two did. Tomato first? One. Then a woman stood up and said 'In Campos, we always sprinkle the salt on the bread before anything else.' This made sense: the traditional industry in this area is sea-salt. The salt flats have been in continuous operation since Phoenician times.

The variations in the order of application of the ingredients have three explanations, to wit: habit (peer-group or family pressure), personal preference (a higher tolerance of olive oil means a greater propensity to douse the bread in it before proceeding) and the understanding of the laws of physics (the roughness of the bread as a factor in the erosion of the garlic or tomato during the scrubbing process, increased by toasting and decreased by the softening action of the oil). To put some pros and cons in plain language:

'If you rub the tomato on first, the bread won't absorb the oil, it just runs off the edge of the slice.'

'If you like oil as much as I do, you pour it on before the tomato, then afterwards as well!'

'If you pour the oil on first, it soaks through the bread, and when you're eating, it drips on to your clothes and stains them.'

'Pouring the oil on first softens the bread too much, so when you try and rub the tomato on, it just skids across the slice.'

Equipment

If you're really starving, no equipment is needed: rip a piece of bread off the loaf with your teeth, dunk it in olive oil and sprinkle some salt on with your fingers. Yet, to have the appropriate instruments at hand and well laid out helps to create an auspicious atmosphere in which to carry out the bread & oil ritual. As for the esoteric aspects—whether the waning moon favours the bread's absorption of the ingredients, whether the thread of oil should be applied widdershins, whether one should be facing east better to tune in to tellurian energies and transmit them to the bread & oil—these will have to wait until the second volume of the book.

To slice a Majorcan loaf correctly, a serrated bread knife isn't necessary. What works best and generates the least crumbs is a large kitchen knife with a steel (not stainless) blade, such as those made in Consell. A wider blade makes for a straighter, more even slice, but if the trajectory is out of true from the start, it makes it harder to correct. Those with more experience, especially peasants, use a *trinxet*, a large pocket knife with a billhook-shaped blade. (It also has the advantage of allowing the experienced user to slice pieces of sausage, cheese or fruit with one hand, leaving the other free to hold the slice of *pa amb oli* at the ready for alternate bites.)

The Majorcan farmer's wife, *sa madona*, always slices the loaf against her breast, never on the breadboard. This has an explanation: it is logical to cut across the thickness (the shortest dimension) of a loaf, and since the diameter of a large round loaf is about five times its height, and considerably longer than a large knife, this would mean balancing the loaf on its rounded edge on the bread board, a very unstable position which could perhaps divert the operation from the kitchen to the surgery. The *madona's* bosom, on the other hand, is a most appropriately soft nook which moulds itself easily around the perimeter of the loaf, and affords it the stability necessary to obtain thin, even slices. Another advantage: the crumbs fall into the *madona's* apron rather than on the floor. For best results, she will use a *trinxet* whose hooked shape helps to maintain a constant pressure of the loaf against the chest while slicing. To obtain the cleanest slice, the loaf shouldn't still be warm; it is better left for a day.

The *setrill* or olive-oil cruet is fundamental if you want a nice, well-controlled trickle of oil on the bread. When a Majorcan pours this thin thread of oil onto the bread, the 'flourish' or line drawn by the oil is as personal as his signature. Casual observation reveals flourishes in the shape of spirals, cross-hatches, figures of eight or zig-zags. A steady flow is fundamental, and the experienced *pa amb oli* maker feels as uncomfortable with an unfamiliar *setrill* as he might with a borrowed fountain pen. The flow is regulated by three factors: the size of the hole in the spout, the intake of air to replace the displaced liquid, and, to a lesser extent, the amount of oil in the cruet.

The spout should begin a little above the base of the cruet (in order to avoid any impurities which have settled on the bottom from pouring out with the oil) and should end in a hole about 2–4 mm wide, according to taste. If the cork is airtight, a vacuum will form and the oil will stop flowing. A little air intake—a tiny vertical v-shaped channel cut in the cork—will compensate for this. The more sophisticated *setrills* have a stainless-steel tube set in the cork for this purpose; the cheap ones have a pop-on plastic lid with a hole in it; in both cases the flow can be regulated by covering the air intake with one's thumb.

There are designs of *setrill* which drip more than others, but some oil will inevitably dribble down the outside. However, if you always keep your *setrill* on a saucer you'll avoid staining your tablecloth. Many households used to keep a tin or clay saucer specially designed for this purpose, incorporating a wire grille placed half an inch from the bottom to keep the base of the *setrill* clear of the sump of accumulated drips.

At one time, the oil cruets in this part of the world were small decorated clay pitchers. Glassware was being made in Catalonia from the twelfth century onwards, but it didn't reach the poorer households until centuries later. Glass *setrills* were a great step forward: not only could you check the oil level at a glance, but blown-glass techniques allowed for a much finer, more sinuous spout which gave greater control in both marksmanship and dosage. By the fifteenth century, as can be seen by inspecting the wills and testaments kept at the Archive of the Kingdom of Majorca, mention is made of the *setrills* which form a part of the *atuells* (household glassware).

According to Andreu Oliver, owner of Can Castanyer, well-established glass and ceramics shop in Sóller, the three most popular designs are the Valencian (cylindrical or square in section, with vertical sides), the Catalan (the most popular, fig-shaped with a very wide base) and the Majorcan (like the Catalan, but more stylized and elongated to a tear-shape). The Majorcan style is now hard to find because it was difficult to adapt to mass-production.

The *setrill* shouldn't be too full (the oil, obeying the law of communicating vessels, will spurt out of the spout if the cruet is filled above that level) nor too empty (the sediment at the bottom might find its way onto your bread).

It's not easy to find a traditional *setrill* in a useful size (about 250 ml). The market seems to be polarized between stainless-steel catering size and the restaurant-table cruet-stand size. There is of course the 'artistic glassware' aimed at the tourist market, but the designs tend to be as impractical as they are beautiful. (The same goes for tourist-oriented pottery: try finding a rustic or artistic teapot that pours properly.)

A *matançer*[1] from Pina described a curious oil cruet to me recently. 'When I was a kid, we used to visit my aunt in Sóller, and for elevenses she'd slice us some bread and then give us each a small green sweet pepper, cut the top off, and pour a little salt and oil into it. We'd bite a little hole in the bottom of the pepper and the oil and salt would flow out onto the bread. Then we'd eat the sweet pepper with the bread & oil.'

I understand that the best salt-cellar ever made was designed at the Bauhaus in the 1930s. It is slightly hour-glass-shaped, with a stainless-steel top which pops off to allow refilling. It is manageable, discreet, simple, capacious and cheap. There are many other models, including salt mills with which you can grind coarse sea-salt directly onto your food. Most experienced cooks will salt a plateful of bread & oil the way they would a large fish, by throwing a pinch of salt at it from a distance and with great force. This assures a proper distribution of the grains of salt, and, for all I know, maybe even charges them with negative ions on the way.

The 'Fine Table Salt' which is sold commercially tends to contain a chemical anti-caking agent to stop the grains sticking together in humid conditions; some brands add so much that a pinch between your fingers trickles away like

---

[1] A freelance butcher who makes house calls around Martinmas, the season for making sausages.

hourglass sand. One way to avoid this interference with your statutory rights is to buy pure fine sea-salt and pour it into the salt-cellar along with a spoonful of dry rice. The rice grains are too large to fall through the holes, will absorb any excess humidity and, when the salt-cellar is shaken, break up any lumps that might have formed.

At any health-food shop you can find natural products which will liven up your bread and oil without pumping up your blood pressure. *Gomasio* is a delicious mixture of salt and ground toasted sesame seeds, and can be easily prepared at home. You can also try celery salt or herb and vegetable salts such as Herbamare (which also contains kelp).

The best way to toast bread, for unmatchable flavour, is over the embers. Failing that, a flat toaster (avoid those with asbestos for safety's sake) or a griddle-iron works well over a gas flame. To toast bread under the grill is an option unexplored by the majority of Majorcans, since this invention hasn't been fully accepted by the housewives of this country. Electric toasters are normally designed for what the Spanish call English Bread, (the Hispanic equivalent of Mother's Pride is called Bimbo), but extra-wide models are now available to accommodate full slices from a one-kilo Majorcan loaf, or half-slices from a proper two-kilo loaf.

I hardly need go into the techniques of toasting bread, of which the British reader is probably a master, except to remind him of the basic precept that more heat for a shorter time gives a crisper outside and softer inside. If a more consistent, drier toast is needed, as may be the case if it is to be subjected to the *pa amb oli* scrub treatment, then turn down the heat (or increase the distance from the coals) and let it toast a little longer.

Storing food:
the *rebost* and the refrigerator

To find out which foods are recent additions to the Mediterranean diet, try the following experiment. Open the fridge door and take out anything that can be kept in the *rebost* (larder or pantry): fruit, vegetables, wine, cheese, olives and pickles, dried fish, eggs, cured meats and sausages. Whatever's left—butter, margarine, milk, soft drinks, beer—is probably a recent import from the colder climates and loaded with calories or cholesterol, or, in the case of fresh meat and fish, the type of food which was consumed immediately when caught or bought.

'It's sad when you realize that today you can't keep a proper *rebost*', says Tomeu Torrens, 'and that's mainly because the climate has changed, but so has the way of preserving food. A loaf doesn't keep as long as it used to, nor do today's *sobrassades*[2] keep half as long as those of my grandparents' day, and that's in spite of all the preservatives which the meat packers unfortunately pour into their products to keep them from going off. It isn't one single factor, it's a confluence of many things: the climate, the ingredients, pollution. Taken to an extreme, we could say that the cow's diet not only affects the taste of the cheese but also its keeping qualities.'

Similarly, a sausage made from pig that is fattened on bags of un-sold-by-date potato crisps that the poor animal has to open with its snout (I swear I've seen it with my own eyes), can't be compared with one made from a local breed of black pig fattened on the traditional diet of broad beans and figs. While on the subject of the effect of an animal's diet upon his posthumous shelf-life, I'd like to

---

[2] One of Majorca's best known exports, a raw pork paté cured with salt and paprika, stuffed into a length of gut.

relate the following curiosity. My father used to mention—
and I don't know where he dug up the fact—cases of
monks and nuns who, wishing to achieve sainthood
(demonstrable through the incorruptibility of the flesh)
devoted their last years to a diet of figs. The phrase 'to die
in the odour of sanctity' underlines this concept.

Traditionally, the Majorcan family pig was raised on
kitchen waste: peelings, cabbage leaves, apple cores, but
never on left-over meat. It's not as if such a thing was to be
found in poor households, but the peasant knew that a
carnivorous pig produced a bleached out *sobrassada* with
poor keeping qualities. The meat industry, in recycling
slaughterhouse offal into animal feed, have made meat
much cheaper for the consumer; in the post-war years a
whole chicken would have cost a Majorcan labourer a
week's wages. Yet this affordability of meat carries a hidden
cost: the health risks which appear with every scandal,
from salmonella eggs to mad cows.

'One apricot can last you a fortnight in the fruit bowl,
and another only five days,' continues Tomeu. 'The only
difference is that the first was picked when ripe, from a tree
in the *secà* (the dry-crop area of Majorca) watered only by
the rain and fed with manure, while the second was
harvested from a tree irrigated once a week and doused in
chemical fertilizer. The second is larger, more attractive, it
looks as if it's about to burst; yet the smaller, runt-like
apricot from the *secà* will contain four times as much
natural sugar and you can be sure it will keep a lot longer.
As for the home-made jam you make with the good-
looking apricot, it won't taste of anything and will have
gone mouldy after a month.

'At our restaurant in Inca, Ca n'Amer, we used to buy
"keeping" melons in September, the kind you hang in

string bags, to serve them up at Christmas. We had to stop because every year they would last less, until it came to the point where they would rot after a fortnight. This is partly because new irrigation techniques have reached everywhere and the *secà* is no longer *secà.*'

Organically grown fruit and vegetables do keep longer. It may not seem so at first sight because chemically treated or radiated apples and oranges may maintain their good looks even while rotting inside. An organic product looks its age, but at least it reflects its interior state. We'll soon be talking about liposuction and facelifts at the supermarket.

A proper larder or pantry is not compatible with an urban lifestyle because it takes up a lot of room. Few people go to the trouble of making jams or preserves, let alone bottling fruit and vegetables or curing meat and cheese. It's much easier to buy cans or jars at the corner shop. Whatever isn't in a tin or glass jar ends up in the fridge or freezer.

'The refrigerator today isn't an indispensable appliance; it's inevitable,' says Tomeu. 'There are so few products generally available that can be kept in a contemporary larder, that you'd end up eating the same thing every day: Inca biscuits and olive oil. But a piece of cheese just out of the fridge has no taste; you have to wait a couple of hours for the room temperature to bring out its full flavour. And inside the fridge, the different foods pick up each other's smell and taste, something which doesn't happen in a well-designed larder.' (Try ice-cubes made in a fridge which they have shared with an open melon!)

'What affects food most isn't so much the heat itself but the fluctuations in temperature. A traditional Majorcan larder in a stone house maintains a fairly constant temperature and humidity, oscillating only some five degrees throughout the year. A larder in a fifth-floor apartment kitchen may vary ten degrees in a day.'

I asked a meat-curer and sausage-maker of the traditional school for his point of view: 'A proper larder or cellar is the best place to keep cured meats and cheeses. The most important thing is that it should be ventilated at two points. The first should ideally open to the outside of the house, be it the patio or the back yard, but it must face north. The other opening can be interior, but it shouldn't face due south because one must avoid a direct draught, otherwise the air won't reach all the corners of the larder. The interior ventilation can be in the form of a *gelosia*[3] set in the wall, or a screen in the larder door. As a rule, Majorcan larders are dark because they are set under the stairs or in a semi-basement under the half-landing and always next to the kitchen.' Sunlight, of course, can harm preserves.

Many people use the fridge to keep food away from insects. A useful alternative is the small free-standing or hanging screened cheese-cage, which can be suspended in a cool, well-ventilated spot.

A neighbour of mine with years of experience as a professional cook, explains that, 'in my childhood, a cabbage leaf was a portable icebox. The fishwives would weigh your fish and then roll it in a cabbage leaf before wrapping it in newspaper. The leaf would keep it fresh and moist until you got home. Today's fridges are too cold for most things, especially greasy foods and cold meats because the cold congeals the fat and makes it unpalatably cloying. A fridge will also dry your food out.

'Cured meats need fresh air. They should be hung up so they don't get mouldy by being in contact with

---

[3] A clay or cut-sandstone decorative grille.

any surface. When a *botifarró*[4] is left on a plate, it gathers a slimy patina that puts you right off it; better hang it from its string.

'Oil and lard are the easiest preservatives to use. If you want to keep pork products such as paté or salted chops, just put them in an earthenware vessel, heat some lard until it melts, then, as it cools but is still liquid, pour it over the meat. The air will be driven out and the lard will set, acting as a vacuum-pack.'

Many foods can be kept for days, weeks or months with no artificial or chemical agents, simply using lard, oil, paprika, salt, brine, sugar syrup or vinegar, which not only preserves them but can improve their flavour.

Before the arrival of refrigerators, we had three ways of keeping things cool in the summer: the icebox, the well or cistern, and, for the lucky few, the *bufador*.

An icebox was no more than a well insulated, airtight chest which would hold a block of ice onto which some salt was sprinkled to keep it cooler longer. With one load of ice, choc-bars and ice-lollies would last a couple of days.

Before a system was invented to manufacture ice, blocks of the stuff would be wrapped in sacks and brought down by mule from the snow-houses in the mountains. These were deep pits into which the ice-makers shovelled snow and trampled it into solid ice, where it would be kept for months before being sawn into blocks. Only the rich had access to ice-cream; most of the ice was used in the hospitals to stop haemorrhages. From the 1920s onwards, it was produced industrially and would arrive in the villages by the daily bus or train, which would have an ice-chest built into it.

Not every house had its own well (tapping into an

---

[4] An individual-size black blood sausage, flavoured with aniseed.

underground spring) or cistern (collecting rainwater). Until the arrival of dynamite, to dig or excavate one, preferably in the bedrock, was a major undertaking that would have to be shared by four or five households. But by the twentieth century, most houses on the island had their own, and each family would take advantage of this natural insect-free refrigerator in the summer months. Fruit and vegetables would be put in a basket and lowered down until almost touching the cool water while melons, watermelons, bottles of wine and soda-water, all scrupulously clean, would be put in a net and lowered into the water to chill.

A *bufador* (literally, a blower) is a natural phenomenon found in limestone mountains such as the *Serra de Tramuntana*, the range which runs from Andratx to Formentor. Cold air from an underground system of caves emanates through a crack in the rock. I know of caves used as cold-storage, and of houses and hermitages which have built their larders against a *bufador* in the bedrock to take advantage of this natural air-conditioning.

'**Bread with bread, dinner of fools.
Bread with oil, meal for wise men.**'

Chapter 3

Roots

When the gods Poseidon, Zeus and Hades, the sons of Kronos, drew lots to divide the world among them, Poseidon was given dominion over the sea. A bit piqued because he had no foothold on dry land, he vied with the goddess Athena for ownership of Attica. This prize was to be given to the deity who could offer the more useful gift to mankind. Poseidon made his bid: the horse. What could be more useful than that? But Athena had an ace up her sleeve: the olive tree. No contest, decided the Olympian judges: the olive tree provides shade in summer, timber in winter, beautiful wood to work with, fruit to eat and an oil that serves as fuel for lamps, as a lubricant, an unguent, as a medicine and as the basis of all cooking. In honour and gratitude, the people of Attica named their capital city Athens in honour of the goddess.

The oleaster or wild olive tree can be found all over the Mediterranean, yet it only produces tiny wild olives, too small to be worth picking. The sweet olive was already being cultivated four centuries before Christ's time in the Middle East, from Turkey to what is now Libya, supposed birthplace of Athena.

In Alexander the Great's time (356–323 BC), while the olive tree planted by Athena on the Acropolis was still bearing fruit, the companionship of bread, oil and wine was well consolidated in Greece, forming the trivet which supported the diet of that age. Thanks to Alexander's conquests, Greek culture—including the culinary—extended from the Danube to the Nile, and, pushing eastward, as far as the Indus delta—present-day Karachi.

The Phoenician traders and Roman legions also spread olive culture. Wherever the oleaster grew naturally, slips of domesticated olive would be grafted onto the hardy stock. One could say that the Mediterranean culture is defined not so much by the shores of Mare Nostrum, but by the presence of the olive tree, which can be found from Portugal to Persia, and on both the European and African shores.

Greek mythology holds that Demeter, the corn goddess, was also born in Libya, so we can assume North Africa to be the symbolic cradle of both bread and oil. The Romans, who worshipped Demeter under the name of Ceres—origin of the word cereal—set their sights on conquering this region with the aim of turning it into the bread-basket of their rapidly-expanding empire, an empire which was opening up to the north and the east and had an increasing number of mouths to feed, not only their legions but also the newly subjected tribes. Greed finally split the sack;[1] 'centralized planning' from Rome demanded more harvests than the North-African soil could sustain, causing one of the world's first humanly-induced ecological disasters. Over-exploitation left the fragile topsoil at the mercy of the wind and rain, much of it silting up the ports and making it impossible to export

[1] Typical Majorcan expression.

the grain. When in the fifth century AD the Vandals decided to head south and conquer the legendary 'bread-basket of the Empire', they discovered precious little arable land left. Finding themselves empty-handed for all their efforts, they decided to annex the more productive Balearic Islands, Sardinia and Corsica.

The vine, originating in the area which today is Armenia, began to be cultivated as far east as India and west as Spain, although the island of Crete is reputedly where the Greek god Dionysus (Bacchus to the Romans) invented wine. The Dionysian wine cult soon began to gain popularity over consumers of other primitive alcoholic beverages, including beer, which was already popular in Egypt. The taste for wine went from strength to strength among the Romans, who extended viticulture outside the Mediterranean area, to Portugal, the Loire Valley in France and the German Rhineland.

The Phoenicians, more merchants than conquerors, had already brought the bread & oil culture to our end of the Mediterranean, exploiting the salt flats in the south-east corner of this island, which are still producing today and must be one of the longest-running businesses in the world. Yet it was the Romans who imposed their trilogy of bread, oil and wine upon the whole Mediterranean area, planting olive groves, vineyards and wheat wherever most suitable—depending on the topography and climate of each zone—and shunting the surplus around the known world according to demand. The Mediterranean ports handled all manner of cargo, from minerals to slaves, but especially provisions. Vessels were loaded with sacks of cereals, oil in clay amphorae—which only a strong man could lift—and wine in wineskins.

It is curious to note that today more than half of the

annual production of Spanish olive oil is shipped to Italy, as it was two thousand years ago. In his gastronomic treatise, Apicius recommends Iberian oil in at least three recipes. And today, as in Roman times, the Italians re-export Spanish oil to other countries.

The importance of the bread-oil-wine triumvirate in the ancient world can easily be perceived through reading the Bible, where these three elements are repeatedly used as symbols, beginning with the story of Noah (the olive-branch in the beak of the returning dove). Olive oil, symbolizing liquid gold, was also used to anoint the kings of Israel. But it is especially throughout the Gospels that these three images recur, culminating in the Last Supper, where bread and wine are chosen to represent Christ's body and blood. Equally, other elements which still form a part of the *pa amb oli* culture also receive a high symbolic charge in Christ's own miracles and parables: fish, figs, grapes and salt. In the Bible, when pork is mentioned at all it has negative connotations, as when Jesus exorcizes the Devils from a Gadarene man and relocates them, at their request, in a herd of two thousand swine, who all promptly trot off a cliff and drown (St Mark, 5, 1-13). The pig was considered an impure animal, a view probably influenced by the danger of trichinosis, a disease to which, among all farmyard animals, swine were particularly susceptible in that time and climate. Christianity has re-established pork as an acceptable food, but the two other great Mediterranean religions—Judaism and Islam—still consider it impure.

Islands of a certain size were surprisingly difficult to conquer militarily in ancient times; they tended to be colonized a little at a time once the invader had consolidated a foothold at one corner. A closed insular society, as in the case of the Balearics, will adapt gradually to the ways of the new boss, but the age-old habits that form the islander's relationship to his environment—diet, cultivation, work-songs, building techniques—tend to carry on unchanged in a pure state within the fabric of popular culture. It's likely that the Roman habits, customs and language took firmer root in the Balearics than in other parts of the empire, for the simple reason that our slingers worked as mercenaries for the Roman army (having done a stint working for the Carthaginians under Hannibal) and thus probably assimilated the Roman culture on campaign as equals rather than as subordinates. With the collapse of the Roman Empire, as had happened with the Greeks and would happen later with the Moslems, its cultural legacy lived on undisturbed in the quiet backwaters of the folk culture of the islands. For instance, according to Antoni Pinya, head of the kitchen in the School of Hostelry of the UIB *(Universitat de les Illes Balears)*: 'The pizza can be traced back to the Etruscans; at the Pizza Museum in Italy, historical research based on archaeological excavations refers specifically to the *portada*, a round savoury tart identical to our *coca de verdures*. What we have here is the authentic pizza which the Romans taught us to make when they settled on the island; we've carried on making it in exactly the same way.

'There are more than 400 recognized ways of making pizza, and 1000 variants of each recipe; everyone has added his own particular stamp. The same happens with *pa amb oli*.

'The other legacy we received from the Romans is the Majorcan loaf, the *pa mallorquí*. We've preserved a purely Roman culinary procedure like a relic down the centuries. If you go over Apicius's book, and local histories of the

Mediterranean, you'll notice how the islanders—Sardinia, Malta—absorb the different contributions made by all the different cultures which have passed that way. Each colonizer imposes his own criteria, laws and customs, and there they stay in one form or another. In the kitchen, there's always a reason behind any habit.

'Throughout the Mediterranean, flour and olive oil have always teamed up. Here we eat them in the form of *coca* and *galleta d'oli*, in both cases, the flour is mixed with oil before baking. The Majorcan loaf contains no oil or salt, so we add it directly on the slice when we make a *pa amb oli*.'

The Moslem colonization of the Balearics in the tenth century didn't introduce new habits so much as strengthen and update the culinary culture which the islanders had inherited from the Romans, Greeks, Carthaginians and Phoenicians. The Arabs and Berber tribe's people who settled here had of course been drinking from the same source as us because North Africa had also formed part of the Roman Empire. However, the colonization of the Balearics wasn't launched from North Africa but from the Spanish mainland, most of which had been under Moslem domination for a couple of centuries, and was flourishing both agriculturally and culturally. The Moslem settlers found the islands in a shambles after successive waves of foreign domination—Vandals, Byzantines, Franks—and put the agriculture back in order. New varieties of olive from their plantations in Al-Andalus (today's Andalucia) were grafted onto the local olives, most of which had probably reverted back to their wild state.

There are no lakes or rivers in our archipelago. Water flows in seasonal mountain torrents, but most of it disappears into the latticework of underground caverns, filtering down to the water-table. If the water was locked into the heart of the mountain, the arable land was almost entirely on the dry plains. The most important and longest-lasting Moslem contribution to the islands was to reconcile the two extremes, as they had done from the Yemen to Provence. On the one hand they brought the mountains' water to irrigate the best farmland by constructing *qanats*—horizontal galleries excavated into the hillsides to intercept and capture underground water—and artesian wells serviced by water-wheels, all complemented by a system of channels to distribute the precious liquid. And on the other hand they brought agriculture to the mountains by terracing the hillsides in order to retain the soil and also to drain the surface runoff, so that the heavy rains would be channelled directly into the torrents and no longer erode the hillsides. Even so, only about fifteen per cent of the islands' surface was actually cultivated. In Majorca, the Arab nobles set up many large estates and palaces in the foothills of the *Serra de Tramuntana*, in which water was the most important element; fountains abounded, cool patios, pergolas, shady walks, enormous stone water-tanks. Every estate and small community had not only a reservoir but a communal bread oven and an oil press. The plain was settled in small villages, mainly by Berber tribesmen, whose names still evoke an Islamic past: Binissalem, Algaida, Muro, Inca, Bunyola, Sóller, Banyal-bufar, Alcudia, Alaró.

On the arrival of King James I of Aragon, *Jaume el Conqueridor*, the vine was still being cultivated here, and it appears that pig-farming was also common; it seems that the Moslems had tolerated the slightly unorthodox customs of the indigenous Majorcans—by now a rich mixture of Balearic, Greek, Roman, Vandal, Jewish,

Frankish, Byzantine, Arabic and Berber blood. The purely Latin etymology of the word *sobrassada*[2] (from *sale presata*, preserved in salt) suggests the annual pig-slaughtering ritual of the *matances*, with all its cathartic and Dyonisic overtones, harks back to the Roman domination, although it must have been done discreetly in a Moslem society. But when King James's successor brought settlers over from Catalunya and Aragon to repopulate the island after the Moslems had been killed, driven out or put into slavery, these homesteaders not only pulled the pork out of the closet but flaunted it almost as a symbol of good Christianhood. It soon became a basic part not only of our diet but also our folk culture: at Martinmas, in November, the family pig is slaughtered and everyone joins in with songs and stories, preparing *sobrassadas* and *botifarrons*, salting the bones, keeping the lard and then celebrating with a big pot of *frit*.[3]

In the fifteenth century, two hundred years after the Christian conquest, the oil boom began. Olive oil soon became Majorca's biggest export and laid the foundations for the wealth of Palma as a trading port, with the help of the Jewish community who ran the business side of things.

James the Conqueror had divided the island among the nobles and bishops who had financed the conquest; they were given the *possessions* (mountain estates), while he kept the fertile plain for himself to rent or sell to the settlers. But the olive groves were mainly concentrated on the poorer soil of the hillsides, so the descendants of these big landowners became immensely rich thanks to this liquid gold. With the use of slaves (brought from the Slavic

---

[2] Some say that the word *sobrassada* and the technique for making this raw pork sausage was brought from Italy in the fourteenth century.

[3] Fried offal and vegetables flavoured with fresh fennel.

countries and paid for with oil revenue) the upper slopes were cleared of oak forests and terraced, following the Moslem techniques, to an altitude of 800 meters above sea level, the limit at which an olive tree is productive. The rockier patches were leased to *roters*, estate workers who could supplement their income with a few jars of oil. The olive groves began to give work (remunerated or not) to an important part of the population: woodcutters, stonemasons, ploughmen, grafters and pruners, and teams of *gallufes*.[4]

Oil presses begin to multiply in all the *possessions* and villages in the olive-growing area, working night and day throughout the winter to deal with the harvest. Many of the original millstones of these *tafones*[5] were still being driven by mules or donkeys up until twenty years ago. The olive and wheat harvest was hard on the peasants too, who lightened their load with the Moorish cadences of work songs such as the *cançó de collir olives* (olive-picking song) the *so de tafona* (olive-mill air) *cançó des battre* (winnowing song) or *so de pastera* (kneading tune). I heard the grandfather of Miquel Oliver, a friend and illustrator, singing them in the 1970s.

Bread, oil and wine had formed a cosy ménage-à-trois for two millennia without anybody sticking their nose in. But the sixteenth century saw the vine, wheat and olive tree exported to the New World and in exchange many new American imports made their appearance in Europe. Among these was an ornamental plant with yellow fruit, which the Aztecs called *tomatl*; but upon arrival at the port

---

[4] Girls from the plain, accompanied by a chaperone, brought in to harvest the olives.

[5] Olive presses.

of Cadiz, the plant was named *mala insana* (unhealthy apple). The leaves were poisonous for farmyard animals, nor did anyone venture to taste the fruit so similar to Belladonna berries. What's more, an Aztec legend prophesied that 'the destruction of the conquerors will come by the hand of the tomato and potato'. Perhaps this was a cryptic reference to 'French fries 'n ketchup' culture, corrupter of our civilization.

The French court chefs, always investigating novelties with which to tickle the jaded royal palates, began to discover the culinary possibilities of the tomato. (Perhaps an attempt at regicide backfired.) The tomato boom had begun. According to Antoni Pinya, 'it was terrible; it shook the whole culinary establishment, not only in Europe, but all over the world.' The Italians adopted it with true passion and called it *pomo d'oro*, golden apple. At this point, most varieties were still closer to yellow than red. By the beginning of the nineteenth century, the tomato began to form a fourth basic element of the Mediterranean diet along with bread, oil and wine. 'The only new ingredient that has really found its way into the age-old cooked flour-and-oil formula has been the tomato.' It joined the pizza and the pasta as a guest artist, and ended up being star of the show.

Over the years, hundreds of new varieties of tomatoes are developed, each one larger, juicier and redder than the last, with finer, shinier skin. Yet there is a fairly primitive descendant of the *tomatl*, small and yellow-orange in colour with a dull, thick skin and not a particularly succulent flesh, which has acclimatized itself perfectly to the dry-crop areas of the Balearic Islands and is perfectly adapted to the dietary needs of the population. It remains in an almost pure state today, and is known as the *tomàtiga de penjar* or hanging tomato, because it has the advantage of lasting the whole winter when threaded onto a string which is hung from a nail in the larder.

INGREDIENTS

Chapter 4

Bread

Pa is the second word we Majorcans learn to pronounce (after *mama* and before *papa*) and probably no other food in Western culture has a greater symbolic charge than bread. It is a synonym for nourishment and sustenance: 'our daily bread', 'earn your bread' (or 'your *sopes*', which is effectively the same thing[1]), 'babies arrive with a loaf under their arm',[2] 'longer than a day without bread…' In this part of the world, the table isn't laid until the bread is on it, however rich the meal that follows. There's an old joke about the Spaniard who ate a whole roast sheep at one sitting. He was asked how he had managed such a feat. 'Oh, it's not so hard if you have some bread to help it go down.'

The Romans paid their wages in salt, giving us the word 'salary', but in the Christian culture it is bread that represents the reward for our toils, charity towards others, and all we need in this life. If you were brought up in post-

---

[1] *Sopes Mallorquines* consists of a vegetable soup poured over thin slices of dry bread, *pa de sopes*, or just *sopes*. On the *possessions*, farmhands would bring their own bread and the overseer would provide the broth.

[2] 'When there's another mouth to feed, something always turns up.'

war Spain, you probably still have the automatic reflex of picking up and kissing a piece of bread that has dropped to the floor. This age-old habit served to ward off the devil, who always sees our clumsiness as a sign of weakness, putting his cloven hoof in the door and leading us into temptation. Keeping a piece of bread at home was also good protection against evil; garlic made it all the more effective. It's probably true to say that for those of us who grew up in this part of the world, bread still maintains an importance as a symbol even though it is losing importance in the kitchen.[3]

Our Mediterranean diet leans heavily upon cereals, but today we eat less in the form of bread—it's fattening, we're told—yet we consume the same quantity of flour in different ways: pasta, biscuits, pastries, sliced 'light' bread, sandwiches, pizza, and hamburgers.

New work habits have changed our dining customs; not only are families smaller but they seldom all coincide for a meal to break the bread together. Today they buy less real bread than a generation ago, but eat even less than what they buy. The idea of throwing any away was almost sacrilegious in our grandparents' time; today we toss yesterday's stale loaf into the bin when we get home with a soft, warm *baguette* from the supermarket. The price of a loaf is laughable when compared to the average hourly wage in the Balearics. If we have lost part of the symbolic value of bread, it's partly due to its having lost monetary value. It used to be normal to recycle stale bread to make *sopes mallorquines*, *pancuit*, *oliaigua*. It would be sliced into cubes and fried as croûtons to serve with lentils, or ground

---

[3] The British equivalent is to throw a pinch of salt over the left shoulder when you've accidentally knocked over the salt-cellar; Old Nick always whispers into your left ear when you've been clumsy, so some salt in his eye keeps him at bay.

into bread crumbs as a topping for macaroni (when cheese was only for the wealthy) or to thicken soups. It could also be used to make *pa amb fonteta*: 'We'd soften the slices in water, then add salt and a bit of olive oil, some people would add some vinegar. Before false teeth became available, this was the only way for the old codgers to eat *pa amb oli.*' And babies too; to quote the thirteenth-century mystic Ramon Llull, in his book *Blanquerna*: 'Infants... cannot ingest solid foods other than *sopes* of bread soaked in milk or oil...'

On the mainland, bread crumbs are used in cold soups, in coating croquettes and fried vegetables, as well as being the basis of shepherds' dishes such as *migas* and *gachas*.[4]

It seems that nobody has time for that sort of thing any more, and in any case the poor quality of most of today's bread doesn't justify the trouble of recycling it. As it's so cheap and tempting to buy a fresh loaf at any time of day, we've lost the habit of keeping bread. The joke is that everybody throws away old loaves and then buys dry bread, at twice the price, in packets of *Tostadas a la Brasa*.

During the 1980s, the consumption of bread bought from the bakery descended an average of three per cent annually, while packaged bread and pastries increased proportionately. Now traditional bread, like olive oil, is slowly beginning to regain lost ground having overcome its 'bad press'.

Pa mallorquí or *pa de pagès* (Majorcan or farmhouse bread)

As the standard of living rises, bread is no longer a 'basic' but a 'complementary' food. We've witnessed the invasion of French loaves and white rolls, as well as more exotic items: rye, soya, sesame, low-gluten or five-cereal loaves;

---

[4] The British reader will of course immediately think of bread pudding.

onion bread, Italian *chapata*, Greek *pita*... each one surreptitiously elbowing the traditional Majorcan loaf off the baker's rack. Mind you, with good marketing the *pa mallorquí* could be touted as a 'low-sodium loaf.'

If a bakery hasn't sold the day's production of Majorcan bread, it can usually sell the surplus to a bar or restaurant because the next day it is as good if not better, as long as it's made in the right way. An unsold French loaf has to be thrown away by next morning; it can be deep-frozen while fresh, but upon thawing out, the crust tends to detach itself.

Why are we turning our backs on the honest, round, consistent Majorcan loaf after a couple of thousand years as the basis of our daily diet, especially our bread and oil? One reason, undoubtedly, is its low social status. There's no lack of modern, urban or nouveau-riche islanders who scoff at this 'peasant loaf', the same people who abhor speaking *mallorquí* and deride all that reminds them of their rural roots. However, the biggest factor weighing against our farmhouse loaf is rather more prosaic: it's a question of size. The traditional size is the nominal two kilo loaf; smaller sizes are commonly available but, as one baker explains 'the surface area of the crust on a half-kilo loaf is out of proportion to the crumb, so most of the flavour and fragrance gets baked out of it.' And, with Spain now having the lowest birth rate in Europe, today's typical household would take a week to get through a proper sized loaf, and that's a problem for a generation unused to chewing.

The truth is that traditional recipes for recycling leftover bread turn out better with the consistent *pa mallorquí* than with the newer varieties, which seem to turn to powder when grated or to scum when soaked. A nearly stale slice of *pa de pagès* will revive when toasted—if eaten at once—and can be given a new lease of life with a bit of olive oil and scrubbed tomato. For recalcitrant cases, you can resort to the old English mother's trick of making 'soldier boys' (I gather that is now the politically correct term) by toasting the slice, cutting it into sticks, and then dipping them into a soft boiled egg or fried egg yolk. The slice can be oiled and tomatoed before being cut into sticks; in this, their gala uniform, these Redcoats can also accompany a dip (*guacamole*, *hummus* or plain tuna and mayonnaise) at a formal reception.

'Thirty years ago, nearly all the bread made in any Palma bakery—not to mention a village bakery—would be large round Majorcan loaves and the occasional *llonguet*.[5] In the large farmhouses and country estates, they would only prepare the dough once a week. Not a crumb was thrown away in those days; that's something that's come along recently.'

So says Toni Mimó, our village baker. If Palmesan snobs turn up their noses at this 'poor man's bread', in the hinterland you're more likely to encounter the opposite view: 'That bread they bake nowadays is good for nothing. Take one of those French loaves made with packet yeast; yes, it'll give off a nice whiff, but by the evening you may as well be eating chewing gum, it's lost all its chirpiness.'

Or this: 'Buy a *baguette* in the morning, by the evening you can bend it in half and it won't snap, and the next morning it's stiff as a board. But real Majorcan bread never goes rubbery; you can eat it the next day or the day after, with oil, with or without ham, or olives or what have you, and it's like honey, know what I mean? And that's thanks to natural leavening and the wood-fired oven. There's nothing like doing things naturally, I always say. The bread

---

[5] An unglazed bread roll made with very elastic dough and shaped like a coffee-bean.

they sell you still warm from the electric oven, it can't do your stomach any good, nor does it satisfy you like real bread. Once I ate a warm *baguette* made from that new-fangled frozen pre-cooked dough, and I thought I was going to die, they sell it to you raw, it formed a lump in my stomach. Maybe if they at least used a proper wood-fired oven…'

The authentic *pa de pagès* is one of the least adulterated items of our basic diet: it only contains flour and water, because the leavening used—known as *llevat mare* or mother-yeast—is simply a piece of fermented dough set aside from the last batch. If a Majorcan loaf is as good today as tomorrow and lasts a week in a cloth bag, it's thanks to the absence, rather than the presence, of chemical preservatives.

The fashion for eating tender warm bread at any time of the day or night was induced as the result of technological and chemical advances in the baking industry. Everybody is now going wild over pre-cooked loaves which need only a few minutes in the oven—or seconds in the microwave—to finish the process. Traditional bakers call it *pa de palla*, 'straw bread'. One can imagine the chemical additives needed to allow the normal baking process to be interrupted, left on hold for hours or months, and then continued, while at the same time convincing the consumer that the finished item is edible. Well, it looks like the consumer is totally convinced (or seduced) if we take note of all the *baguetteries, croissanteries* and other 'piddleries' which have been springing up all over the place thanks to the twin miracles of pre-cooked dough and zap-'em electric ovens. But this instant bread isn't limited to the world of fast-food and TV dinners; it's been discovered as a useful fall-back for normal bakeries that have a small turnover. Gone are the days of knowing your clients' daily needs and baking to meet the demand, anticipating the local school outing by preparing an extra couple of dozen *llonguets*. But today's market in Majorca is fickle, especially in the dormitory towns; even in small villages you never know if you're going to end up with a load of unsold stock or whether an early-morning swarm of Belgian cyclists in Martian outfits will descend on the bakery and leave the rest of the villagers without any breakfast. So, to have a secret supply of ready-made French loaves, rolls or *croissants* in the fridge waiting to be browned in the oven at a moment's notice certainly increments the baker's 'capacity for commercial reaction' which is so valuable in today's unpredictable market. The twelve hours needed to make a *pa de pagès* or an *ensaïmada* —mix and knead the dough, let it rise and bake it—seem to belong to a bygone era of regular clients with dependable habits. A lost world.

Well, not totally lost. A village baker protests: 'The other day a salesman tried to sell me some frozen *baguettes* which were kneaded and shaped two months ago! They can read me all the sermons they like, but they're way out of tune.[6] It's like going out hunting thrushes or rabbits and then sticking them in your deep-freeze: they've got to go straight into the pot, there's nothing else like it. Christmas cakes taste best at Christmas. Even if you make them the same way but out of season, they won't rise or taste as good. For every thing there is a season, like *esclatasangs*.[7] If you're talking green beans, the early ones are the best.

---

[6] 'They can try and convince me but they're barking up the wrong tree.'
[7] 'Blood-bursters', a highly prized wild mushroom that appears after the September rains.

If you're talking *botifarrons*, they taste better the colder it gets. *Cada cosa a son temps, i a s'estiu xigales!*[8]

Wheat

Wheat was traditionally grown on the plain, but it was also cultivated on the mountain estates which needed to maintain their self-sufficiency—a very important concept among islanders. On the lowlands, wheat was ground by windmills, but in the mountains and foothills, the mills were driven by the seasonal torrents or diverted spring-water.

Wheat can be sown between the olive trees, since the two harvests don't overlap. Take a hike anywhere along the *Serra de Tramuntana*, and wherever the wind blows hardest you'll find an *era*, a threshing floor. This is a large flat circle about twenty-five metres across, where the harvested wheat is threshed (beaten to break open the husks) and then winnowed (tossed in the air so that the wind blows away the chaff, leaving the wheat grains to fall back on the ground). Within a few minutes walk of our village there are five threshing floors; I've even seen an *era* at an altitude of 800 metres, on the small plateau close to the peak of the Teix. On a mountain hike you'll probably also come across some smaller, slightly convex circles in sheltered spots; but these are *sitges*, charcoal-burners' circles.

Today the olive groves are no longer dedicated to two-tier farming; it's no longer worthwhile to sow wheat or broadbeans for fodder beneath the trees. Even on the plain, wheat cultivation is also disappearing because the farms are too small to be able to compete with cheap imports. Majorcan wheat is grown as much for fodder as for flour.

The Gomila flour-mill in Montuïri specializes in

---

[8] To every thing there is a season, and to the cicadas that's summertime!

grinding flour for Majorcan bread and for making *panades* (Easter meat pies). One of the Gomila brothers tells me that the typical Majorcan varieties, *blat barba* (bearded wheat) and *blat mort* (dead wheat) are still cultivated on certain large estates on the plain.

'The grain is a lot larger than the standard varieties; it's tastier than imported wheat and gives a nice colour to the bread, but if you don't mix in some foreign wheat with it, the bread turns out too dense for today's tastes. In the old days they used to mix in some *xeixa* which is a finer local variety, but today we use foreign hybrids which are grown locally. Sometimes a farmer will bring in a sack or two of Majorcan wheat to grind for his own bread; up until recently there were some hermits[9] who would bring us their wheat for their own consumption. But the wheat grown on the island, both the autochthonous varieties and the hybrids, aren't enough to begin to meet the demand; it's nearly all shipped in.'

Flour

'Local flour?' chuckles a baker: 'The sack says *Harinas Mallorca*, but just take a look where they built the mill: it's on the quayside. There's not enough local wheat to fill your pipe, it all comes from Lerida.

'The real *pa de pagès* is made without yeast; it's simply flour, water and natural leavening which is made by leaving some of the previous batch of dough to ferment. The flour can be white or brown; the origin is the same, but to obtain whiter flour you just pass it through a finer sieve to filter out the husk or bran, and the wheat germ. All that's left is the starch.

---

[9] There are still several Catholic monasteries and hermitages on the island, dedicated to the contemplative life; all are more or less self-sufficient.

'You normally get three grades of flour: for white bread, for brown bread *(pa moreno)* and for *pa de sopes* which is darker than the brown flour. But the flour for *sopes* they send us now, in sacks that say *SOPES* and *AL GUSTO MALLORQUIN*, is far too white. Why? Because it's made by *forasters*.[10] The foreman says, "Hey, you, put a bit of brown flour into that batch, it's for the Majorcans." But he's never tasted a plate of *sopes* in his life. And the flour they send us for the *pa moreno* is even whiter.'

If all the goodness of the wheat has been extracted from the white flour—the vitamins, proteins, fibre and minerals, which account for thirty per cent of the weight—what are the advantages? First, it's more homogenous and therefore easier to work. Second, it keeps better because it's not worth any insect's while to get into the sack if there's nothing of value inside; a bag of wholemeal flour, on the other hand, will soon be alive with teeming micro-organisms and creepy-crawlies. Wheat keeps longer as a grain than ground; until one sack of flour was finished, another of wheat wouldn't be taken to the mill. During the lean years, to preserve the quantity of food counted for more than quality; and since lean years were more frequent than fat ones, so was the habit of eliminating whatever it was that attracted pests. This explains why white flour and rice is still so much more common than brown, in spite of modern preserving techniques. A different problem, which modern technology hasn't yet solved, is posed by the wheat germ. Once milled, the wheat germ—the most nutritious part of the grain which contains the vitamins

---

[10] Balearic islanders divide everyone else into *forasters* (outsiders), *estrangers* (foreigners) and *catalans*. The prevailing attitude is as follows: the *estrangers* don't know any better, the *forasters* should know better and the *catalans* know too much for their own good.

necessary to metabolize the starch—soon oxidizes and turns rancid, affecting the whole batch. The great majority of supposedly wholemeal flours available today contain no wheat-germ; the only solution is to grind your own grain in a domestic grain-mill just before using it, or to add stabilized wheat-germ flakes to your bread & oil.

Mixing the dough

In the old days, every kitchen had a *pastera* or kneading-trough, a kitchen table whose hinged top lifted up to reveal a deep tray, with sloping sides, beneath. In this trough, a piece of left-over dough would be placed on a saucer of oil and covered with a cabbage leaf to stop it drying out; in the darkness of the closed *pastera*, it would be left to ferment all week. When baking day came round again, this 'mother-yeast' would be used as leavening for the new batch of dough, which was mixed and kneaded in the trough and then left there to rise, with the table-top down to avoid draughts. If the weather was cold, a charcoal brazier could be placed underneath to help the process.

'The action of mixing and kneading draws the gluten out of the flour;' Toni explains. 'This is what gives the dough its elasticity, and consistency to the bread. The more you mix, the better the final texture of the loaf; it takes more effort to draw the gluten out of wholemeal than white flour. The brown flour we use for *pa moreno* is neither white nor wholemeal, but somewhere between. It contains more nourishment than the white flour and is more workable than wholemeal flour. Real Majorcan bread is different from other kinds because it's made without salt or yeast. A loaf made with natural leavening keeps much better, and the lack of salt also keeps it from going stale so soon because it doesn't crystallize.

'If you leave a mixture of flour and water alone for a few days, it will begin to ferment, and that's what you use instead of yeast. If you use a piece of the last batch of dough, the process is faster, although not as fast as packet yeast. Mix the "mother" into the new batch, leave it overnight in the *pastera* to ferment, and the next morning you shape the loaves, let them rise again or "prove", and they're ready to pop in the oven. It's a slow process; it takes its own time to rise; the same when we make an *ensaïmada*, which is also a two-day process. There's no two ways about it: if you want to have an *ensaïmada* ready in an hour's time, you can't call it an *ensaïmada*. Today everybody goes for quick results, they'll simply toss in a bit more packet yeast, and that's why things turn out the way they do. People still make Majorcan bread, but if you want it the way it used to be made, you won't find it easily; everybody used to mix the dough by hand, bake it in a wood-fired oven... the dough for the *pa mallorquí* was the first to be mixed and the last to be baked. It had to rise for ten or twelve hours, and you'll not find anybody willing to accept that sort of workday.'

It's very hard to find bread mixed by hand with 'mother-yeast', unless it's made privately at a *possessió* or maybe a vegetarian restaurant or health-food shop. One of the few bakeries, if not the only one, where you can find this kind of authentic Majorcan bread is Ca Na Fiola, in Bunyola; it's run by Margalida '*Fiola*' and her son Joan, a strong man in his late thirties. It's hard to interview them together as they both talk at the same time. Let me allow them to take over the story, as I try to unravel the voices.

Joan: 'When I leave this business, we'll close down; in any case, you're not likely to find anybody else willing to mix dough with his bare hands or work these hours.'

Na Fiola[11]: 'Kaaaa! Nobody's willing to do anything anymore except get paid...'

Joan: 'People come all the way from Palma; 'It's not true,' they say. 'I can't believe they still mix the dough by hand!' That's all right by me; anyone can come over and see me do it.'

Na Fiola: 'Some people are in a hurry to grow old so they don't have to get their hands dirty. They don't want to lift a finger, but the soul gets no benefit if the body doesn't work.'

Joan: 'You have to get used to doing this kind of work, you're handling quite a few kilos of dough. In every ovenload, there's fifty loaves, and we have to fire the oven four or five times a day, one after another. You're always on the go, and you have to rob a lot of hours from your bed because everything must done before anyone else is awake. I don't think any other bakery on the island does the whole process by hand.

'In the north of Spain, in a half-abandoned mountain village, there are some youngsters who have restored a bakery and they sell their bread in the nearby town. A man who works in the savings bank around the corner happened to go there on holiday and he told them that he liked real bread but that it was hard to find nowadays. And one of the kids says:

"Well, it's strange that, living in Majorca, you haven't been to Bunyola to buy bread.'

"What? In Bunyola? That's where I work!'

"Well, in that village there's an old lady and her son

---

[11] Most rural Majorcans are referred to by their *malnom* ('bad name'), since there is a limited repertoire of Christian names and surnames. Despite having originated with the nickname of some ancestor, the *malnom* is identified with the house (*Can* or *Ca Na* is the equivalent of the French chez) rather than with the family itself. Thus, Ca Na Fiola is 'The God-daughter's House'.

who make bread by hand, without any additives, and there's a mystery there because their loaves rise as if they were using industrial yeast!'

'I don't know what the secret is; it must be the way I mix and knead. I only use tap water, the same flour as everybody else and a bit of yesterday's dough. Some people say we use soda-water and God knows what else, but that's nonsense. You're only allowed to use mains water because it's regularly inspected, or well water if you take it to be analysed every so often. Our set-up here doesn't follow the regulations to the letter, but we're allowed to carry on as we are, simply because this bakery is historic. The rules say you can't even build a wood-fired oven any more. If you're mixing dough by hand and something falls in by mistake, you find it at once; but with one of those cement-mixers they use nowadays, you'd be looking forever!

'I've seen this enormous chap on TV kneading two loaves at the same time, one with each hand. Very impressive. However, industrial dough is a lot easier to work because it's full of chemicals and a lot lighter. But when it's baked and you want to cut a slice, rrrraaaaack! It falls to bits. I see they've had to invent a breadboard made of wooden slats with a tray underneath to catch the crumbs, because the bread you buy today doesn't slice, it shatters.'

Na Fiola: 'Making bread isn't complicated; the only complication is in doing it properly. Baking runs in my family. Take Joan here, and then take my brother who runs the other bakery in town and has more baker's blood in his veins than Joan. A son of mine and a brother of mine, I love them both the same—well, perhaps I love Joan a little bit more—but just one mouthful of bread and anybody in town can tell who made it. Why, Lord, why? The same flour, the same *pastera*, the same oven? Because my brother is always in a hurry, and if you're in a hurry you can't do anything properly.'

Joan: 'You have to go easy, *tira-tira*, now you turn it around, now you turn it over, now you stretch it, if you work the dough properly, it doesn't stick to your hands. The phone rings and you can pick it up without having to wash your hands. You can't finish mixing the dough too soon; it takes as long as it has to take. In twenty minutes I make a *pasterada*, but you put a novice to work and he'd take two hours to do the same amount of work. You learn on the job.'

Na Fiola: 'You have to serve your apprenticeship. When you're teaching, it's the old codgers who know the most. Nowadays they turf the old folks out on the street and give the young 'uns the teaching jobs, but they don't know their arses from their elbows, and so everything goes to the bloody dogs. But didn't the old codger know more than all of the rest put together?'

Letting the dough rise

For bread to be sponge-like, the dough has to have risen (fermented and inflated) before being put in the oven. Other than the 'mother yeast' or natural leavening already described, there are two raising agents normally used in baking: fresh or dried yeast (a fungous by-product of the sugar industry, dried and pressed into cakes or in powder) and baking powder (bicarbonate of soda, used mainly for biscuits and cakes).

The mixed and kneaded dough should be left to rise to double its size in a warm place (ideally, the *pastera* with the lid down), protected from any draughts and not allowed to dry out. The slower the process, the better the result; fresh yeast works four or five times faster than natural leavening.

The dough is then 'knocked back'—kneaded again to get rid of the air bubbles—and divided into pieces of equal weight. These are formed into round loaves and placed within the creases of a floured cloth to 'prove' by doubling in size again. The time needed depends upon room temperature, which, if the bakery has a wood-fired brick oven, is pretty warm all day long. When the loaves have risen, they are flipped over so the smooth side, which was in contact with the cloth, becomes the top, and the 'ugly' or wrinkled part is now the bottom, which tends to pick up some ash from the floor of the oven.

Baking

'You're still allowed to use a wood-fired brick oven, the Moorish oven as it's known here, but once you convert it, legally there's no going back. Isn't that lovely, to have it all automatic: push a couple of buttons and off it goes. With a big Moorish oven, there's the job of finding the wood and lighting the oven, and once you've finished, scrape out the embers, sweep it out and finally scrub it clean with wet sacking tied to the end of a long pole. Get real! Who's willing to do that kind of work and slog those hours? Nearly all the Moorish ovens now run on gas, fuel oil or electricity. Neither affects the taste of the bread, for better or for worse, but a loaf baked in a wood-fired oven bloody well has to taste better!'

The only bakeries that continue to use wood are family businesses, because hiring and insuring outsiders to do the job would be prohibitive; the working hours are incompatible with either a normal family timetable or with the night life of the majority of young Majorcans.

The igloo-shaped oven has to be fired with bundles of pine branches, which are in plentiful supply as long as the woodlands are cleaned of brushwood to prevent forest fires. This kindling is put inside and lit with the draught open. The vault begins to heat up, the flames then appearing to dance on the 'palate' or ceiling of the oven; when it is hot enough, it turns white. Then heavier branches are pushed in and as they burn to become embers, the oven floor heats up. A handful of flour tossed in serves as a thermometer: the hotter the oven, the quicker it will burst into flame. When the balance has been reached between the heat of the vault and of the floor, the embers are raked to the perimeter, the loaves slipped in on bread paddles and the mouth of the oven closed. The insulation packed around and above the vault—stones and sand from the torrents, shards of clay brick and tiles—helps to maintain an almost constant temperature for hours. If the oven is used every day, it never cools down completely. The baker knows how to control the temperature by the way he distributes the embers, which part of the oven takes longer to heat up and which part maintains it longer. Experience allows him to play with the differences between heat radiated by the floor and ceiling, the mouth and the back of the oven, depending on whether he is baking bread or *coca*, *ensaïmades* or *panades*.

'Bread can be baked with steam or without; steam gives it a bit of lustre. You stick a French loaf into an electric oven, then voom! you give it a blast of steam and it picks up that nice shine. And the more steam you give it, the prettier the glaze. But Majorcan loaves and *llonguets* come out completely matt, dull: the oven has to be dry, the chimney open to let out any moisture that might have built up. You lose some heat, but that's the way it's done.'

Selling bread

If you want to be well-informed of what's happening about town, don't enquire at the Town Hall, don't tune into the local radio bulletins, just drop by the bakery first thing in the morning and you'll get the news hotter than the *ensaïmades*. The bakery has always been the nerve centre of the village or neighbourhood. There's one in Secar de la Real, just outside Palma, which was about to be torn down twenty years ago to make room for a housing estate. All the local inhabitants organized a protest (unheard-of in Majorca) to defend it. Now that the figure of the *saig* or town crier has disappeared from rural life, the role of broadcaster of municipal news has been assimilated by the baker or his wife. If the church bells are tolling, the baker will know for whom.

'Majorcan loaves aren't subsidized,' Toni grumbles, 'but the price is regulated. A baker makes more on a French loaf than on a Majorcan one. I'd be a lot better off if I didn't have to make any *pa mallorquí*!'

'The Baker's Association gives us guidelines so that we price our loaves more or less the same, so there should be little difference from one village to another. A client comes in and says, "Give me a kilo loaf of *pa mallorquí*." He takes it home, puts it on the kitchen scales and it only weighs 700 grams! So he says, "The bakers are robbing us blind!" But that's not true. There's never been such a thing as a real two-kilo loaf, or one, or half-a-kilo loaf in Majorca; those are just convenient names, the standard sizes date back to an older system of weights. There's an official minimum weight and maximum price established by the Balearic Government; an inspector makes a surprise visit, finds a loaf that weighs ten grammes less than the official weight, and *cataclac*! they dish you out a big fat fine for breakfast.

That's why we do as we're told.'

Na Fiola: 'Before, we used to make loaves which were called kilo or two-kilo loaves, but they weren't really; a few years ago they were standardized into 330 grammes, 700 grammes and one-and-a-half kilos. But one of our small loaves looks ridiculous next to a small loaf from another bakery which has a lot more volume, because everybody else makes their *pa mallorquí* with a lot of air.

'We're protected by Saint Pancras here. All bakeries tend to have their figure of *Sant Pancraci*, even though he's not the patron saint of bakers: in Majorca, *Sant Honorat* has that job. But anywhere they sell bread, especially in the area around Sineu, there's always a figure of Saint Pancras. He should never be without his sprig of parsley, which has to be facing him; it brings a lot of luck. Saint Pancras brings you gifts; he's a very good saint.

'We sell to half the world; people come from half an hour's drive away and take five or six loaves for the week. Maybe they don't eat the lot themselves, but there's one woman from Sóller who comes in on Wednesdays and carts off a dozen loaves; she and her family eat the lot, they don't sell any off to anyone else.

'We also make *panades*, *robiols* and things like that, but since everybody likes our bread so much, we concentrate on that. Nobody buys a two-kilo *pa mallorquí* from an industrial bakery, because if any is left over the next day you can't get your teeth into it. If we have any loaves left over, the restaurants are only too happy to buy it because the next day it's better for making *pa amb oli*. They have to put business first, and their customers want to eat good bread, in thin, well-cut slices. A loaf that's just been made doesn't slice quite so well.'

Slicing and keeping

Na Fiola again: 'A well-made loaf makes no crumbs when you slice it. The custom here is to slice with a *trinxet* against your chest, not on the table. This way you can slice it as thin as you want, as long as the bread has cooled down because no-one's ever cut a decent slice off a warm loaf. There's a bar on the square, if we only have warm bread they'll get through at least five loaves but if the bread is yesterday's, three loaves will do them fine. With the crumbs you get from a modern loaf, you have to sweep the floor afterwards.'

Joan: 'To keep a loaf properly, it's important not to leave the bread on the table, it's the air that dries it out. Also, be sure to keep it out of the sun. As soon as you've finished slicing you should wrap the loaf in a tea-towel and put it away in a drawer or a wooden cupboard, it will keep better than in the larder. I've eaten one of our loaves after two weeks kept in a cloth bag in a drawer, and it was still edible, and hadn't a spot of mould on it.'

Other vehicles for *pa amb oli*

While the purists insist that Majorcan bread has no substitute as a base for an authentic *pa amb oli*, the success of the *llagosta*[12] and its acceptance among the urban population suggests other possibilities, such as the Italian *chapata* [*ciabatta*] bread (which is now beginning to appear on the menu in some of the more irreverent *pa amb oli* parlours), brown sesame rolls, whole-wheat and even whole-grain ('five cereal') loaves. Toni explains: 'The *llonguet*—basic ingredient of the *llagosta*—arrived from Catalonia, but it's well established in the islands. The dough

---

[12] A toasted *pa amb oli* sandwich made with a *llonguet*. See page 182.

is similar to French bread, but the procedure is completely different. It's made by hand, nobody's invented a *llonguet*-making machine yet. You take a piece of the dough, flatten it until it's really thin, then roll it into a sausage, more or less oval in cross-section. Then you cut the sausage into narrow slices and lay them on their sides, so they rest on the cut surface, on a well floured baker's cloth. You gather the cloth into parallel creases so the *llonguets* don't touch each other as they rise. When they're well proved and soft to the touch, just before they go into the oven, you take a sharp knife or razor and make a deep cut lengthways. Then as they bake they open up along the slice and take on that characteristic coffee-bean shape.

'I like Majorcan bread for my *pa amb oli*, but when we started also making these German-style wholemeal loaves, I tried putting oil on it; I don't know, maybe I like it even better and all! A lot of my customers also use it for their bread & oil, and they say it's too much! I learned to make it years ago when I was visiting a German friend over there. I was the only baker in Palma making this kind of bread, I had the proper flour sent from the mill in Kulmbach, and it's really expensive. Now other Spanish mills have jumped on the bandwagon and offer their German-style flour at bargain prices, but like anything else, you halve the price and you halve the quality.'

Galletes d'oli (Inca biscuits[13])

Antoni Pinya loves getting to the bottom of any culinary riddle, but in this case he touches a patriotic nerve: 'The *galleta d'oli*, commonly known as *galleta d'Inca*, has Anglo-

[13] If you've visited any Majorcan village shop or hypermarket, you've probably seen racks full of plastic bags of savoury Inca biscuits in all their varieties: normal, wholemeal, salt-free, gluten-free, bite-sized, and school-packs (six

Saxon roots! Once, while the Royal Navy lay at anchor in Palma harbour some 150 years ago, the quarter-master general ordered a consignment of ship's biscuits from a Majorcan bakery. The baker kept the recipe and adapted it to our local ingredients.'

He was probably from Inca, and his delicious adaptation of the infamous British ship's biscuit found itself a comfortable nook in our local diet.

As Tomeu Torrens explains, 'in Inca it's very common to eat your *galleta d'oli* scrubbed with tomato and a few drops of oil, as if it were a miniature *pa amb oli*. A five-year-old can easily prepare one all by himself: he doesn't need a knife to split open the biscuit. Also it's great if you like garlic, because the surface is rough enough to sand down a whole garlic clove.'

In the years before the Balearics could boast their own University, Majorcan students normally had to go to Barcelona or Valencia to further their education. In the cheap seats of the Trasmediterrànea ferry, they could be easily identified: in one hand they would be carrying a big *sobrassada* and in the other a huge bag of Inca biscuits.

Footnote 13 continued:

biscuits and a bar of chocolate). The most popular brand is Quely. The name is said to have originated with the founder's infatuation with Grace Kelly, although *galletes d'oli* are also made in many small bakeries in or around the town of Inca. They are normally about an inch high and slightly oval in shape, the perfect size to get your thumb and index finger around. Flat on the bottom and with a slight dip on top where they've been pricked with a fork before baking, they are a standby in any Majorcan home. With a well-aimed tap on a table edge they split neatly in half.

Chapter 5

Oil

The bells are tolling as in mourning.
In mourning dress, the countryside;
The fallen olives too, in mourning,
Carpet the ground and the hollows hide.
The nimblest women pickers' fingers
Dart and peck at the fruit below
While in the cauldron, water's boiling,
The pressman dries his sweating brow;
The mill is turning, the press-beam creaking
Into the vats the oil doth flow.

A beautiful land is the Isle of Majorca,
The richest orchard man can know!

(Fragment from *Mallorca* by Tomàs Forteza, published 1932)

PA AMB OLI
Because of the rain of black tears
the mountain solitude is broken.
Country families, singing
& shouting, come with ladders,

wicker baskets & gunny sacks.
Seagulls soar up over and attack
the groves like shopping mobs gone berserk!
Thrush, escapees from Siberia, bounce snacking from
tree to tree.
We too, hopping & singing, going crazy,
with aching back & stained knees,
because the bright green river is flowing
down at the olive press
in the town—our own oil!
A little garlic rubbed on the bread
a pinch of salt & this glory poured on!
By the time the oil lamp is lighted
all have gone home to fire, water & treetop.
Then she & I are two,
three with the great silence
of the occasional falling drop.

(Ralph Cardwell, 1995)

'Olive oil is an essential part of Mediterranean civilization; it even has sacred aspects.' Its honeyed colour, especially when made from ripe olives, earned it the name of 'liquid gold'; in the ancient world, it was valued so highly that it was used to anoint royalty. Olive oil gives us nourishment, medicine, light, beauty and (as a preservative for food and a guardian of health), longevity.

'We consider the olive tree to be the symbol of our Mediterranean culture, and in our diet there's no substitute for its fruit,' declares Antoni Pinya. 'There's hardly any part of our culinary heritage in which olive oil doesn't play a major part; seasonings, dressings, sauces… it is a basic fat and now we have discovered that it's a tremendously healthy one, at that.

'Other cultures spread on their bread whatever fat they have to hand—butter, lard, fish fat. It's a question of habit. Here what we have closest at hand is olive oil whereas in Scandinavia, for instance, the fundamental source of fat is the salmon.'

Eighty per cent of the global production of olive oil is centred in southern Europe. The rest is produced in North Africa, the Middle East and the parts of Australia and America with a climate similar to ours. Today, half the olive oil in Europe is produced here in Spain, even though the EC is loath to admit it because most is marketed as 'Produce of Italy'. For the moment, the oil production in the Balearics is negligible, and mainly for private consumption; it's more profitable to sell the olives for pickling than to gather them for oil.

Olive cultivation

The vegetation on Majorca's terraced hillsides hardly changes colour with the seasons. There are several shades of evergreen: the dark holm-oak forest, the vivid pines which sprout on any untended terraces, the grey-green olive groves which flash silver when the strong winds turn up the undersides of their leaves; and among the olives, the occasional broad-leaved carob tree.

Our olive groves have drifted into the realms of what some Majorcan farmers derisively call *hobby farming* (sic). We've reached this point because it's not worth a peasant's while to become a registered olive-grower and pay the corresponding social security if he and his family are only going to gather a few sacks of olives in the best of years. It's hardly worth it even to pick up a few subsidies to repair any of the centuries-old stone terraces that collapse. What really subsidizes the continuing existence of the olive groves is our seasonal tourism. Most Majorcans from the *serra* who work in the hotels and restaurants, sign on the dole in November and have all winter to spend looking after their olive groves and go hunting, as well a doing a little moonlighting on the side. If the harvest were in summer, all the olives would rot on the ground.

Spain's olive groves produce forty per cent of the world's olive oil and represent 146,000 permanent jobs as well as temporary labour to the tune of 46 million day's wages a year. Economically speaking, Majorca's share of the oil business is negligible. Not only does the size of the smallholdings make them unprofitable—property is usually divided up *ad absurdam* between heirs—but the local topography limits the kind of mechanization that you see in parts of Andalucia. There's no way you could get a tractor with a tree-shaking attachment up the Moorish steps of the Barranc de Biniaraix, nor could you manoeuvre a crop-dusting plane between those crags. Throughout the Mediterranean, the olive is a crop which, in spite of mechanization, gives work to entire families and is responsible for preserving the social fabric of the mountainous regions, culturally as well as economically. If the olive groves were to disappear, the rural exodus would be catastrophic because no other crop can be cultivated in the mountainous areas. At least, for the moment, no legal crop.

'Here at Olis Caimari, we bottle virgin Majorcan olive oil, but we have to mix it with oil from other regions because the local production is so small. We reckon that production will pick up again soon because a lot of young olives are now being planted. We ourselves are setting up plantations on the *pla*, seven thousand trees so far, transplanting local stock but using mainland methods of cultivation. The problem in Majorca is that nearly all the olive groves are in the mountains. At one time, when labour was dirt cheap, there was no problem because for a pittance you could hire olive pickers, but today that's impossible.'

'Before the olive production was mechanized,' a farmer tells me, 'Majorcan oil could compete with the best in the Mediterranean. There were estates which would hire a hundred *gallufes*, women olive-pickers brought in from the *pla* or even from the mainland. The olives were so valuable that if any had fallen into the brambles or a crack in the rock out of the *gallufa*'s reach, the overseer would whittle a stick to a sharp point so she could spear them one by one.'

Olive cultivation in the *possessions* or large estates was based first on a slave economy, later on serfdom, and then (until the tourist boom) on the exploitation of the fact that an island's work force can't afford to look for work elsewhere. After a couple of decades of plunging olive oil prices (due to bad press and cheap imported sunflower and soya oil) they began to steadily rise in the 1980s, and today a litre of Majorcan oil fetches double what is paid in Andalucia, due to the demand for local produce. But even so, it doesn't begin to pay for the labour-intensive work of picking olives, maintaining the dry-stone terraces, ploughing and pruning the trees in the high groves which are accessible only by foot or donkey.

A farmer on the dry part of the Majorcan plain, the *secà*, at one time would have also had a few olive trees to supply his family with oil. But in the nineteenth century, as the phyloxera disease wiped out the grapevine across Europe, any olive trees were uprooted to make way for vineyards, because our vines were disease-free and the demand for wine let the Majorcans name their price. The phyloxera finally arrived here, but by then Europe was being replanted with resistant American vines. Almonds were becoming a big cash crop, so many vineyards were replaced by almond groves, which need as little water and attention as olives. Almonds had been cultivated on the island by the Arabs, not so much as a crop as for their winter bloom; the almond blossom in January is still a tourist attraction. Now we've come full circle and olives are returning to the plain after many centuries, thanks to the new techniques of grafting, transplanting, irrigation and small-scale mechanization. It will soon turn a good profit unless EC plans go ahead to uproot all Spanish olives in excess of our 'official' production, i.e. those trees whose oil is bottled as Italian produce.

The olive tree is at its most productive between 15 and 150 years of age; the trunk then begins to rot from the inside. Yet the roots are still strong and healthy and keep on extending outwards, pushing up new vegetation. Where there was once an olive tree a few centuries ago, today you'll find a ring of five or six mature trees with a common root system. Bulldozers are now capable of transplanting a fully grown olive tree, like the one which is now outside the Palma Town Hall, adding a touch of distinction and 'instant ageing' to any park, square or garden, and skipping the usual fifteen-year wait for fruit.

'Olives from one grove can render more oil per kilo than those from another nearby, but there will be little difference in taste or acidity; that depends more upon the climate. Another variable is the altitude; after a certain point, quality decreases as you climb. Oil quality is usually on a par with the degree of acidity; the more acid the oil, the rougher it tastes. Yes, it *does* have more flavour, it's what we're used to, but it's not the kind of flavour which a good oil should have,' says Gaspar, a professional oil-taster from the Sóller Cooperative.

Another native of the valley, Pere Colom, a young farmer and poet from Fornalutx, goes further. 'The *olivars de sol naixent*, the groves that receive the sun's first rays, tend to produce more oil-rich olives, even if they don't look any juicier. Also, the olive trees protected from the sea air produce more.'

For quality and quantity, then, the ideal olive grove should be protected from the salt breeze, face east and be at an altitude of between 500 and 700 metres, with well-pruned and irrigated trees.

In the pruning season, the branches must be burned on the spot or carted well away, to avoid the trees being affected by the borer. This insect lays its eggs beneath the bark of the dead wood; having hatched out, the young attack any olive tree nearby and blemish the fruit. The borer isn't the only pest with a taste for olives:

'The thrushes have always been hunted here, mainly because they eat the olives. There was a time when the landowners used to pay people to go and hunt thrushes; now they charge them! Professional thrush-catchers were called *llovers*; they used to make *lloves* or traps to catch the birds. A *llova* is basically four stones placed in such a way that one is held up with a stick. A worm is put in the centre of the trap, and when the thrush hops in to eat it, the stone falls on top of it. There was a *llover* from Fornalutx who had over a thousand traps set up all over the mountainside, and every day he'd make his rounds checking up on them. Depending on the wind and the weather, he'd have a good idea of which traps might have caught a thrush.

'A thrush loves to eat olives, even the tiny wild olives,

and he prefers to pick the mature fruit off the ground and then fly off to the forest to eat it in peace and quiet. At one time, seagulls would only feed on olives if the sea had been too rough for them to fish for many days. But lately they're hitting the olives even on calm days; perhaps the sea has been over-fished and there's not enough left for them. A friend and I once killed a seagull when we were kids, we opened him up and there were a dozen olives in his craw! A thrush only eats one at a time.

'That reminds me, once another friend of mine comes up and says: "I just saw a thrush I've never seen before."'

'And I says: "And what makes this thrush so special?"'

'And he goes: "Well, he had an olive in his beak, another in each claw, and another under either wing!"'

'That's amazing!"' I says, completely intrigued, "but how could he fly like that?"'

'"Got you that time, bird-brain!" he laughs.'

Olive picking

'The degree of acidity is set by the olive, there's no part of the process at the oil-press that can affect it,' explains Gaspar, shouting over the noise of the newly-imported Italian machinery at the Sóller Co-op oil-mill. 'Olive oil must be one of the few products which has absolutely no additives. You can't mix anything in with it. Every year it's different; some years the acidity is higher, nobody knows exactly why. The weather may have been exactly the same as the year before, the trees are pruned the same way, given the same fertilizer, but the oil is different from one season to the next. This year, the harvest of '97-'98, the oil is really good, it's a fine year.

'Here on the island, ninety per cent of the olives are picked off the ground; the Majorcans only knock them off

the tree if they have to complete the *trullada*.[1] No other
fruit is harvested off the floor, it's always better straight
from the tree. On the mainland they pull the olives straight
off the branches, they're a little greener and the oil they
produce has a fruitier smell, a bitterer taste. It's a bit spicy
and has a lower acid content; this is the extra virgin oil, the
best there is. The green olive—in fact it's neither green nor
black but mottled—produces less oil but the quality is
better. It's best to beat or comb the tree; you can do it
mechanically or with hand-held rakes which don't damage
the branches.'

It seems that the habit of picking green originated in
the northern Mediterranean where the olives had to be
harvested before the frost set in. In southern Italy they tend
to gather ripe olives from the ground, while in the north
they pick them green. Many Majorcan inventors have
come up with contraptions to gather olives off the ground,
yet whether the principle is suction, a brushing action, or
a spiked roller, no mechanical picker seems to be able to
distinguish this year's juicy olives from last year's shrivelled
ones… or from sheep's droppings.

'The Majorcans are used to an oil which can reach four
or five degrees of acidity and that's what they're after
because it's tasty, but it's the musty taste of an olive that's
been on the damp ground too long. We're telling the
members of our co-op to put their olives in crates instead
of sacks where the air doesn't get to them, where there are
bacteria. That's when the olive gets spoiled, it ferments and
the acidity increases.'

---

[1] 250 kilos, the amount needed to fill the *trullada* and the minimum quantity
required for your own separate pressing. Any less means having to share with
another client whose olives might be of worse quality than yours, and divide
the resulting 80 to 100 litres of oil.

In medieval times when strong olive oil was set aside for preserving food, recipe books would recommend adding honey to counteract the excess acidity. In this century, in the post-war years when even the sharpest oil was better than none, a bit of sugar on your *pa amb oli* would stop the oil grating at the back of your throat.

'Here people pick olives the same way they did a hundred years ago. You could say that if Majorcan oil hasn't the quality of the mainland oil it's partly because here the problem is the terrain, it's not easy to get the olives to the press quickly. Even in the old days, in all the oil presses, the regulars had their own bins where they could empty their sacks until they had enough to warrant a pressing. Maybe it would take a fortnight to gather a full *trullada*, by which time they had already begun to pick up a bit of mould.

'It's not only the way of picking which is different on the mainland; there, the trees are smaller, younger, in a lot of places they are irrigated. If they watered the Majorcan trees, they'd produce a bumper crop every year. Here the trees are too tall; it's not the trunk that bears fruit, it's the younger branches that give you the most olives. Of course, if you're used to picking them off the ground, you can't afford to prune the trees low or you'll keep banging your head on the branches.'

But on islands where arable land is at a premium, farmers tend to try and get the most out of the available soil, and our two-tier farming system demanded that the mule and plough also had to be able to pass under the trees. The olive being an evergreen, the low branches had to be pruned to afford some light and ventilation to the ground-floor crop. And although today nobody ploughs so often nor so close to the trunk, our concept of what an olive tree should look like remains unchanged. The grotesque shapes of our trees is due to their age, and the fact that most of the original trunk has rotted away; I have also heard an 'as above, so below' theory suggesting that the visible tree reflects the roots' tortuous search for water.

'Little by little we're beginning to convince people to adopt more rational methods, but properties are small, people pick mainly for their own consumption, they're not so interested in achieving high quality. If they want to sell their oil, the lower the acidity, the better price it can fetch; but around here it's not a business, it's done on a family basis. You know, "let's round up a few friends to help us get in the olives this weekend". The productivity factor isn't crucial.'

Gathering olives off the ground can be, for someone unaccustomed to this work and to the damp winter climate of the *serra*, an ordeal for the knees and kidneys. Every basketful of four kilos of olives renders a scant litre of oil; not much to show for an hour's work poking about between damp shrubs and under thistles for the evasive little chappies. Many of us who still go for gathering from the ground have found we can save a lot of time by using a strimmer to clear the grass under the trees a week or so before the olives change colour. To go olive picking as a family outing or in order to spend the weekend with friends is a profitable way to commune with nature, each according to his humour. You can work in a group chatting away, but it is equally conducive to solitary meditation.

Why don't we follow the rational northern method of knocking the olives down as soon as they begin to turn colour and thus only have to pick once instead of our weekly pass under the same tree? Well, a Majorcan would say that the only way of ensuring the olive is ripe is to wait for it to fall to the ground... but the hidden argument is that beating or combing the trees not only gives you a crick in the neck, it's also harder work than gathering off the ground. Besides, we've always done it this way and, as they say in the southern US, 'if it ain't broke, don't fix it'.

The *tafona* or oil press

Not so long ago, every *possessió* and large farm with olive groves had its own oil press; today there are still one or two private *tafones* still in working order, but most have been turned into garages, restaurants or rural hotel dining-rooms. Smallholders would go to a commercial *tafona* to have their olives pressed; of these, only four still operate on the island. The oldest, which only opens if it's a good year, is in Caimari on the eastern slopes of the *serra*. The other three are in Sóller and press nearly all the olives on the island: Can Det and Can Repic open according to demand, while the Cooperativa Sant Bartomeu has the most modern facilities and the most work.

Each commercial *tafona* has its particular clients, whose custom stretches back generations, consisting mainly of those whose olive groves were on that side of town, an important factor when transporting by donkey cart. Today the difference between one press and another is only a ten minute drive through town, but habits die hard. Now that none of the large farms use their own mule-powered presses anymore, customers bring their olives to Sóller from all over the island: Andratx, Pollença, Selva... both smallholdings and large *possessions*.

How does, or did, the traditional oil press work? The first operation, after sifting out any leaves and stones, is to crush the olives on the *jaç*, a flat circular bed about a metre high and three across, fashioned out of a single piece of local stone. A contrivance consisting of a wooden funnel connected to a conical millstone, rotates on a vertical axle set in the centre of the stone bed, driven by a blinkered donkey or mule (in Tunisia, a camel) which walks round and round the *jaç*. The sorted olives are tipped into the funnel, the *tremuja*, which feeds them, a few at a time, into the path of the rumbling *trull*.[2] A *trull* can consist of one, two or even three millstones linked together, and the term is normally used to refer to the whole caboodle, including the bed; thus, a *trullada* is a full load of olives, about a quarter of a ton. As the olives are crushed to a paste, the *trull* pushes the dark sludge outwards into the gutter which runs around the rim of the *jaç*. From here the virgin oil seeps out of the paste and trickles into a vat.

'The olive contains more water than oil. What flows from the *trull* is pure olive juice, the true virgin olive oil, a mixture of oil and water. When I was a little girl I used to go to school in Estellencs,' remembers Maria Riera, 'and there was a *tafona* in the village where they'd make oil. The *tafoners* would let the schoolmistress know the day before a *trullada*, and we'd all troop in with our slices of bread, and they'd toast them over the coals. Then they'd take the toasted bread with a pair of tongs and dip it in the oil which had just come out, and it was so good... it was delicious just like that, you didn't even have to put salt on.'

Antoni Pinya explains that 'in the *possessions*, at the end of the working day when the olives had been crushed and were ready for the hot pressing the next morning, a bottle of virgin oil would be collected from the *trull* for the *Senyors* of the estate. This was the best oil, but because of the water content it would quickly become rancid, so it had to be consumed immediately. After the token bottle

---

[2] *Trull* also means noise, uproar or general partying.

had been given to the landowner, all the paste left on the *trull* would be shovelled into a stone vat, the *esportinador*. Then the *madona*—the overseer's wife—would roll up her sleeve, make a fist and stick it into the paste up to her forearm. As she took out her arm it would leave a good sump-hole in the olive paste, into which more virgin oil would seep overnight. The next morning, when the fire was alight to boil the water for the second pressing, the *tafoners* would toast their bread and dunk it into the oil that had gathered in the sump. This was the *tafoner's* breakfast, the *rien-ne-va-plus*, the Number One in the world of bread & oil, known as *pa amb oli de tafona*. From this moment on, the oily and aqueous elements of the olive juice are separated, and in the second or "scalded" pressing, the oil is modified by its contact with hot water.'

At Can Det the olives are still crushed by this traditional method using a double millstone, although the mule has been replaced by an electric motor. In the other two commercial mills still operating, the Co-operativa and Can Repic, the olives are no longer crushed by a stone *trull* but by a mechanical grinder.

Can Repic is an old stone building that stands in a yard off a narrow Sóller side street. The floor, walls and cast iron machinery gleam with a patina of oil; the pre-war grinders and presses still run on 150 volts, like the Sóller train. Trolleys are pushed along tracks set in the floor and olives tipped into the grinder which shudders into life when Miquel throws the switch.

After the 'cold pressing' comes the hot or 'scalded' pressing. In a traditional *tafona* this is done under the weight of an enormous wooden beam, weighing well over a ton: one end of the beam rests on the ground while the other end is raised and then lowered—by means of a

vertical wooden screw, turned by arms of the *tafoners*—
onto the tall stack of circular esparto mats, *esportins*, spread
with olive paste. As the beam is lowered, one *tafoner* 'scalds'
the paste by ladling hot water onto the pile; it seeps down
through the mats, drawing the oil out of the paste.
Meanwhile, his mate watches for any sign of the pile
buckling or bowing, like a spring under pressure; if the
stack begins to twist or curve outwards, he uses a long pole
to push it back to the vertical. In a more industrial set-up
like Can Repic, this hard work is done by hydraulic
presses, but some people still refer to hot-pressed oil as *oli
de bigues*, 'beam oil'.

'We add hot water from this boiler here to the olive
paste, which helps the process of extracting as much oil as
possible from the olive', says Miquel Arbona '*Repic*'.[3] 'All
the paste is scalded with hot water to help separate the oil
from the solids during the pressing. The paste is scooped
up by hand and spread onto these circular mats called
esportins or *caputxetes*. They used to be made of esparto
grass, but now they're made of coconut fibre and polyester.
I suppose the esparto grass ones are no longer competitive,
besides which they are thicker; you used to be able to get
200 kilos of paste between those mats in one pressing, but
with these new ones you can press 250 kilos at one go. The
esportins have a cuff around the edge, they hold the paste in
and stop it squeezing out the sides under pressure; the
caputxetes don't have one—a cuff, that is—they're
completely flat. But as long as the olives are good, not past
it, the paste doesn't squeeze out, so you can use the
caputxetes which take up a little less room. What we do is
spread the paste over the mats—and under the cuff if we're

---

[3] *Repic* means a ringing or chiming of bells.

using *esportins*—then stack them in a tall pile. The stack of mats goes under the press, then we pour hot water over it and apply pressure. All the liquid that comes out—water and oil—is poured, still hot or "turbid", into the *olla*; a different "pot" for every pressing and customer.'

Having pressed the paste under a beam or a hydraulic press until it will yield no more liquid, the process is still not over. The dry paste is scooped out of the *esportins* and thrown back into the *esportinador* where it is beaten with more hot water. The mats are again spread with this rehydrated paste and submitted once more to the heavy pressure treatment, doused with a continuous flow of boiling water to extract that little bit more. The oil obtained by this pressing is known as 'seconds': the quality is lower than the first hot pressing because the continuous heat destroys the vitamin E content as well as part of the flavour and bouquet.

In a traditional press, the 'turbid' liquid extracted from each pressing would be left in the *olla* for hours or days until it had separated into four distinct layers: the 'clear' oil which floats to the top, then the denser 'thick' oil which contains some impurities, and beneath that, the water which has no use.[4] Any solid grounds will sink to the bottom of the vat. The traditional way of pressing olives produced several qualities of oil, from the virgin pressing for the immediate use of landowner's family, right down to the 'thick' oil from the second or third pressing, which was used for making soap, lubricating cart axles and for treating woodwork. Today, any low-grade oil is simply sent off to be refined.

---

[4] But: 'Waste water from olive oil production could be an abundant source of cheap natural preservatives for food and cosmetics, say researchers in Italy, …it is rich in powerful natural antioxidants called phenolic compounds.'(*New Scientist*, 21 August 1999, p.16)

In a modern oil press, however, the process is quicker, as Miquel *Repic* explains: 'The scalded oil is left to settle in a vat for an hour and a half, until it begins to separate from the water. Then we send it through a centrifuge to finish separating the two elements much faster. In the old days, it was done with a lot of patience; the best oil was carefully ladled off the top until the thicker oil was reached. The most logical thing would have been to simply drain the water and impurities out of a hole in the bottom of the vat as we do now, but I suppose there was a risk of losing your oil too.'

The centrifuge has two outlets, one for the waste water and the other for the golden oil which flows, still a bit cloudy, into the customer's own jerry cans or bottles which are then labelled 'first' or 'second' pressing. Today most people bring along ten- or twenty-litre polythene drums, but many still keep the family's four-gallon glass bottles protected by wicker- or cane-work.

Miquel *Repic* fills a glass with the water which flows frothily from the centrifuge and, to prove that not a trace of oil is left in it, lets a drop of oil fall into the glass. The drop doesn't spread over the surface as it would if the water still contained any oil, but stays floating in the middle of the glass.

The Co-operativa Sant Bartomeu is another world. It used to use the same system as Can Repic until a couple of years ago, when it invested in expensive new Italian machinery, which doesn't press or scald the paste at all. This is a modern continuous system in which the olives enter the building though one conveyor belt and the dry paste leaves by another; unlike Can Repic or Can Det, inside the Co-op there's no clue as to whether the gleaming machinery is making oil or packing condoms. The olives are cleaned and then pass through a grinder and the paste stirred or beaten; warm water is added if necessary and the paste then passes directly into a very powerful and noisy centrifuge. The din is deafening, so Gaspar and I go outside to talk, standing next to a still-warm mountain of dried olive paste which is being picked over by some pigeons. When dry, the paste can be burned in the brazier or wood stove.

'What we produce here can truthfully be called cold-pressed virgin oil, because we add the water at no more than 35° centigrade. The olives are ground and the paste is centrifuged without going through the press at all, the oil is separated from the paste and from the water. It's a lot quicker, cleaner and more convenient than pressing the paste. In the traditional method, what can most affect the taste of the oil is when the *esportins* haven't been properly cleaned between one pressing and the next; leftover bits of paste can turn rancid.

'We've made a point of trying to make the people around here more aware of oil quality, by organizing four[5] courses and workshops. The fact that we now bottle some of the local production has helped to push up the price of the local wholesale oil as well; it's doubled in price in five years, and that means it's more viable to pick olives than it used to be. The trouble is that the farmer sells his oil at this high price without taking into account the acidity or the quality; if he's got oil and you want oil, you'll be asked to fork out seven or eight hundred pesetas a litre. The new law which allows the farmers to sell oil up to 3.3° of acidity is great for them. It's only here in Balears that you can sell such strong oil to the public. The thing is, I find we're also losing quality.'

---

[5] Again, meaning 'a few'.

When the oil emerges from the centrifuge, whether the paste has been pressed beforehand or not, it is always a little cloudy. It continues to clarify over a period of weeks or months, the impurities settling on the bottom of the container, and until it has completed this process in its own time, the oil can't be commercially bottled. However, there are many Majorcans who appreciate their oil still *tèrbol* on their bread, in the same way that the Galicians drink their wine *turbio* with seafood.

'The Majorcan virgin oils—that is, the cold-pressed oils—are very good, but owing to the variety of olive and the situation of the olive groves, the acid content is quite high, which is why we have an exceptional ruling that allows the sale of up to 3.3°,' says the managing director of a local company that imports and bottles oil.

'A strong Majorcan oil can be of better quality than one half as acid from certain parts of the mainland, although of course there are other regions which have excellent oils. When we're talking wine, usually more degrees means better quality; with olive oil, it tends to be the other way round, especially when it comes to using your oil for frying.'

Gaspar from the Co-op is adamant: 'On the mainland they make better oil than we do and they do it a lot cheaper, at half the price it costs us. But to the Majorcans, anything produced locally has to be better. To make their *pa amb oli* they want an oil of four or five degrees. Here at the Co-operativa we've made oil of less than one degree, but there's so little of it that it's not worth bottling. However, with what we bottle up to a maximum of two degrees, we keep the shops supplied all year.'

The British tycoon Richard Branson has shown interest in bottling the oil produced at Son Bunyola, his *possessió* in

Banyalbufar, under the name of Virgin Oil, but it's not clear whether the British market is ready for strong Majorcan stuff, even in such tiny quantities. If not, the Virgin Touch beauty service (which he offers to his clients at Virgin Hotels and first-class passengers on Virgin Airways) could use it as a massage oil.

The oil-taster's scorecard

The method used for tasting olive oil is similar to that for wine tasting; the oil is warmed to about 30° centigrade and presented in a blue glass container so that the oil's appearance should not influence the taster's impressions. The oil is sniffed first, then the aroma is inhaled deeply. A teaspoonful is rolled around the mouth and tasted, then air is sucked in between clenched teeth to bring out more subtle hidden flavours. The oil is finally swallowed, the taster taking note of the effect on the throat and then wait-ing to detect the aftertastes. The oil's acidity comes from its fatty acids which aren't water soluble and therefore can't be detected by the tongue, but they can rasp at the back of the throat to the point of making a neophyte cough.

'The taste of an oil doesn't always bear any relation to its acidity; take a Borges Blanques for instance, a good Catalan oil; it only reaches one degree of acidity but the taste is as strong as if it had four or five,' says Gaspar. 'On the report sheet, the taster notes down the positive attri-butes and the defects of an oil. On the positive side, we start by noting the "fruitiness" of the olive. It's better if the olive is green, it gives off a stronger smell; if made from ripe olives, the aroma is a little more subdued. The taster can note down overtones of apple and almond—I've tasted oil with a distinct flavour of raisins, it's quite rare but you do sometimes come across it—but almond is the most appreciated. Other positive characteristics include the taste of newly mown grass, and also green leaves.'

The leafy taste may come from the olive itself being too unripe, or from actual leaves and twigs that went through the mill.

'We also come across the "bitter" or harsh taste; here on the island they'd refuse any oil which is the least astringent, but oddly enough, that slightly bitter note is often considered a good thing. If the oil is made from green olives, it should have a bit of *pic*, a pungent peppery bite in the back of the throat. When you eat the oil with bread, you don't notice the bitterness nor the pungency; you can only detect them when you taste the oil on its own. Then there's the "sweetness", not a sugary sweetness, more of a mellowness which is characteristic of ripe olives and of our Majorcan oils.

'Among the defects we can include traits such as "sour", "winey", "vinegary"… but we don't usually find these in our local oils, nor "roughness", a pastiness in the mouth, either. A "metallic" taste can have been absorbed by the oil when it has been standing in a metal vat, because olive oil absorbs any flavour you care to put nearby. Leave an open bottle of eau-de-cologne next to the *setrill* without a cork, and a few days later you'll be eating your bread & oil and it'll taste of perfume! Another defect is the "musty" taste you get when the olives are left out in the rain or stored in humid conditions and begin to get fungi. The taste described as "hay" comes from some of the previous year's dried-out olives having got into the pressing. "Fusty" is the taste you get from the olives being left too long in sacks and fermenting, which happens here quite a lot, the same as the "rancid" taste which is the worst defect. Any oil will begin to go rancid after a year; this is a process of oxidation, but the more acid it is to start with, the more you notice it. Here we're used to eating our oil a bit rancid. When a Majorcan farmer says he wants his oil to be nice and tasty, what he's really talking about is the sum of all these defects. I can understand that some people like it like that, you can't change their minds. The only positive attribute that a typical Majorcan oil will get on the score card is that it's "sweet" or mellow.'

'The sediments are another story. This is the stuff which the oil picks up on its way through the machines—bits of olive skin, very fine impurities—which can affect the taste if the oil isn't decanted first. If the oil is recently pressed, it'll be cloudy until the impurities settle, so that doesn't help the taste. Once the oil has cleared, it doesn't improve with age like wine; it will eventually turn rancid.'

'Every virtue or defect gets a score on a scale from one (hardly noticeable) to five (hits you in the face). With these scores you can get a pretty good idea of the quality of any oil.'

But in the final analysis, a good quality oil is one where none of the defects is noticeable and no single positive attribute dominates over the others.

Categories of oil

Virgin oil is the first, mechanical extraction from the olive; in Catalunya it's called *oli verge* although on the islands we say *oli verjo*. According to the Alcover-Moll dictionary, it is the oil 'that flows from the olive paste with very little pressure, and without having scalded it with hot water.' True virgin oil is, then, pure olive juice, the most delicious but also the most ephemeral extraction, and for practical purposes we can file this definition away under 'anecdotal'.

Olive oil is classified following two parameters: the

quantity of free oleic acid it contains (the degree of free fatty acidity) and the method of extraction. Although the International Olive Oil Council hasn't settled upon a fool-proof system of classifying something so subjective as the 'quality' of olive oil—a definition as personal as that of wine—they come up with four basic working categories of virgin oil. These are 'Extra Virgin' (less than 1°), 'Virgin' (up to 2°), 'Ordinary Virgin' (2° to 3.3°) and 'Lampante Virgin' (over 3.3°). This last category, favoured by many Majorcans, is 'not suitable for consumption without refining'. The Balearic Government, taking into account both local tastes and local olives, as well as a desire to regulate an otherwise illegal situation, allows Ordinary Virgin oil to be sold over the counter under the name *oli de tafona*, whereas in the rest of Europe, it is only used in small quantities to add colour and flavour to bland refined oils.

Unlike us humans, an oil can be a 'little bit virgin'. To qualify as virgin at all it must be extracted only by mechanical means, with the help of warm water, but without specifying the exact maximum temperature. It's generally agreed that a 'cold pressed' oil shouldn't be subjected to heat extraction, that is, a temperature higher than 40°C.

Non-virgin oils are those which have undergone the heat treatment and/or have been chemically refined.

'Refined oil doesn't taste of anything; what they do is take a bad oil and take out whatever good it might have had: aroma, taste, colour.'

Some of the elements which are beneficial to human health are lost as well; in fact, refining olive oil eliminates most of the advantages it has over other vegetable fats. You won't find pure refined olive oil sold commercially, it would be too bland.

'What they sell officially as "Olive Oil", is mainly refined oil with a little bit of virgin added to put a bit of colour and flavour back in.'

By far the greatest quantity of olive oil consumed in the world comes under this label. The proportion of virgin to refined oil in the mix varies in different countries and regions, to cater to local tastes. Several Majorcan companies—Caimari, Balle, Roselló and Bellver—bottle 'Olive Oil' for the local market, mixing refined oil from the mainland with a dash of local ordinary virgin oil *al gust mallorquí*. Of all vegetable fats, 'Olive Oil' is the most stable at the high temperatures needed for frying. Since olive oil increases its acidity as it heats up, to be fit for cooking it should not exceed 1°. But to use Extra Virgin oils for this purpose would be a crime!

The cheapest olive oil for frying, with no claims to fame, is refined 'pomace oil', *oli de pinyolada*, made from the grounds of the olive pit, the last chance for the olive to give up its soul after being ground, pressed, scalded and centrifuged.

Most of the Lampante Virgin oil, which was traditionally used for such purposes as oil lamps, soap and lubrication, is now sent to the refinery. 'We send our second-grade oil to the mainland and there they refine it and sell it', says Gaspar. 'There's no refining facilities anymore in Majorca, the turnover is too small for it to be worth anybody's while.'

The last refinery on the island closed twenty years ago. I remember as a lad venturing into that enormous dark warehouse in Sa Pobla, carrying some *garrafes* of our oil to be refined so we could use it for frying. Trying to find my way through the gloom, I stepped into an uncovered hole in the floor and almost went feet first into an oil tank.

Not all virgin oil is bottled or refined; a considerable part of the production is used in the manufacture of cosmetics, Japan being one of the most important buyers of Spanish oils for this purpose.

Buying virgin oil

If you want to buy direct from the farmer, by the gallon, ask at the *tafona* if they know who's got some to sell. I have seen some unlabelled bottles of *oli de tafona* for sale in health-food shops at exorbitant prices.

Up until now, there are only two local oils commercially available, both pressed and bottled in Sóller and aimed at the urban or foreign market, in elegant glass bottles. Can Det has recently begun to sell their own Ordinary Virgin or *oli de tafona*, while the Co-op has been marketing a Virgin Oil for a few years now under the name *Olis Sóller*. There is no local Extra Virgin because the few litres which manage to fall below 1° aren't worth bottling separately.

Since Olis Sóller proved that people were willing to pay more for a local Virgin Oil, everyone else has jumped on the bandwagon. But demand is greater than supply, so virgin oils from the mainland are put in fancy bottles with Majorcan names: *Gust d'Oliva*, *Gust d'Oli* and *Oli Verjo*. Olis Caimari has one upmarket brand of Extra Virgin oil, which contains a small percentage of oil pressed from Majorcan olives, in the old *tafona* in Caimari. Even the Co-op resorts to bottling mainland virgin oils when the local harvest is poor—'we don't want to leave our retailers in the lurch'—but when it does, they change their label from *Olis Sóller* to *Olis San Bartolomé*. This ambiguity will soon end when our oil bottlers are finally granted their own mark of origin, 'Oli de Mallorca'.

Now you can find dozens of Extra Virgin oils with their mark of origin (the equivalent of a *denomination contrôlée*) in delicatessens or the gourmet section of the Corte Inglés, such as the famous Catalan *Borges Blanques* or the Andalucian *Calasparra* and *Baena*. (One *Baena* oil, the *Nuñez de Prado*, is particularly tasty and rates a mere 0.2° acidity.) In the health food shops you can find excellent cold-pressed ecological oils, such as the *Oliflix* from Tarragona.

Don't forget to keep your oil in the larder, protected from the light and well stoppered to avoid it absorbing the taste of other foods, air-fresheners, cleaning fluids and the like.

Medicinal Oils

The curative and cleansing properties of virgin olive oil have secured it a place in traditional medicine; it is used both internally and externally. There are people who can quaff half a glass of oil in one gulp without blinking; others feel queasy at the mere thought of swallowing a teaspoonful. The skin, however, always accepts olive oil gratefully thanks to its chemical similarity to our own body oils. The drier the skin, the deeper it will penetrate. There are other finer, less pungent skin oils such as those extracted from the sweet almond or apricot pit, but none has as many health-giving properties as olive oil, which also serves as a vehicle for other medicinal extracts. We've seen how it absorbs the aroma of whatever is nearby; it also absorbs, much as alcohol does, the taste, aroma and curative properties of the medicinal plants which are steeped or macerated in it. All over the Mediterranean we find ancient remedies which use olive oil as a way of helping the skin or muscles absorb those properties. In the

Balearics, for instance, the folk pharmacopoeia contains many oil-based liniments and unguents which treat external problems (stings, bites, rashes and burns) or internal ones (sprains and muscular problems). Some local liniments have absorbed the curing power of plants—the most popular is *oli de Sant Joan* or *de pericó* (St John's Wort or Hypericum oil)—and others of animals, such as *oli de serp* (snake oil). There is even *oli de neu*, snow oil, which is made by filling a pot with newly fallen snow and pouring olive oil over it. The oil apparently fixes the curing power of the ice crystals—perhaps the electrical charge of the ions—as they melt. The oil is then decanted and used as first aid in curing burns.

But pure olive oil is a remedy by itself, and not only found in witches' broom-cupboards. Many paediatricians prescribe a few drops of warm oil in the ear to treat ear-ache, or internally to clean the digestive tracts of intestinal parasites. (Take a teaspoon of olive oil with five drops of fresh lemon juice, repeated daily if necessary until the worms make an exit by the back door, or once a month as a preventive.) If you find a tick on your pet or on your child (often around the ears), don't try and pull it off. The tick will leave its claws and perhaps even its eggs in the skin. First, you must make it loosen its grip by smothering it with a couple of drops of olive oil; within a couple of minutes the tick will suffocate, relinquishing its hold. (Be sure then to throw it on the fire or burn it with a lighter; crushing it won't destroy the eggs.)

You only have to shake hands with someone who handles a lot of oil (an olive picker, a *tafoner* or a kitchen boy) to appreciate its effect upon the skin; they all have very smooth hands. Oil has always been used as a beauty treatment, not only to clean the skin but to give it more lustre and elasticity. A good *pa amb oli* eater won't clean his hands on a rag afterwards; he'll rub the excess oil into his skin. Some Andalucians use it as an after-shave balm and moisturizer.

Olive oil is the basis of many traditional beauty treatments such as hand creams and facial masks, body lotions, bath oils and hair conditioners. When I was a child, suntan lotion was hard to come by on the island so the foreign residents would mix their own using one part of lemon juice to two of virgin oil; I'd prefer to smell like a salad than like a branch of Boots any day. The sun block factor could be augmented by adding a few drops of iodine from a bottle, or by soaking some *posidonia* (the most common Mediterranean seaweed) in the oil first. Olive oil was also useful on the beach for removing from your feet the gobs of tar that washed up on the shore.

I heard someone quote the following anecdote from Mort Rosenblum's book, *Olives: the Life and Lore of a Noble Fruit.* Jean Calman, a 121-year-old Frenchman from Arles was asked how he had reached that age in such good health. He replied: 'Olive oil is present in all the dishes I eat, and every day I rub it into my skin. I only have one crease, and that's the one I'm sitting on.'

Self-medication with bread & oil

Here's a tip from Joan Frontera, 'Jeannot': 'In the event of having had too much to drink, eat a slice of bread soaked in virgin oil and in an hour's time you'll feel right as rain again. You can get rid of a hangover with a good tablespoon of neat oil, but it seems that the bread helps to absorb the excess alcohol in the body and calm the stomach cramps that tend to go with this concurrence of symptoms more effectively than Alka-Seltzer.'

There's nothing better to treat a case of 'Monday-mornin' blues, one of dem what don't let you put on your walkin' shoes' and get to the corner chemist's. According to Dr Benito, a Majorcan specialist in bowel cancer, 'For someone who has indigestion or diarrhoea, the best thing is a little boiled white rice, grated carrot or a well-toasted *pa amb oli*.'

I know which I'd choose.

In Mika Waltari's historical novel *The Egyptian*, there is a scene in which the main character has to poison another. In order for the victim to suspect nothing, the poisoner would have to eat the same food. The only way he can protect himself from the mortal poison intended for the other is to first drink a small bottle of olive oil in order to have his digestive tract well lubricated and protected from the poison's mortal effect.

The trick of the preventative dose of oil might also work to protect yourself from that important business client who wants to get you too drunk to read the small print, but whom you can't afford to offend by refusing a drink.

Oil soap

'With the olive oil that was too strong or rancid to eat, my grandma used to make soap at home, mixing it in a bowl with ashes, caustic soda and *pega grega*.[6] When it set, it was cut into pieces like a cake and we used it to wash the laundry, not just our hands,' says Pere Colom. 'This soap did as good a job as the detergents they sell today—for washing linen, we'd add some *blavet*[7]—but it did no harm to the trees or to the vegetables. The water that flowed

---

[6] 'Greek pitch' or coal tar.
[7] Reckitt's blue.

through the public wash-houses went on to irrigate the orchards without doing any damage, and however much the water dashed about as it flowed down the *siquia*, it never frothed. But irrigating your trees with water from a washing-machine is as good as poisoning them.'

Another popular use for inedible oil was to mix it with ground, hot red pepper and rub it into beams and furniture to treat them against woodworm.

Oil to burn

In this part of the world, everyday (or everynight) lighting used to depend mainly on oil lamps. Before paraffin-wax candles became common, they were made from beeswax and were only used for religious purposes or by the aristocracy. A poor family would use a simple lamp made of a square piece of tin pinched at the corners to form a tray, like an ashtray. From each corner a wick would stick out, burning steadily while drawing the oil up from the bottom of the tray. It would smell and smoke more than a candle, but it gave off a reasonable light, especially when hung against a white-washed wall. A more elaborate version was the brass oil table-lamp shaped like Aladdin's; some were decorated and sophisticated to the point of having polished brass reflectors and up to a dozen wicks.

'Whoever handles the oil, greases his palm.'

Chapter 6

Tomato

A *pa amb oli* without tomato is like... is like... well, it's just a tomatoless *pa amb oli*. Relax, it's not the end of the world. In the Balearics, and everywhere else in the Mediterranean, we'd been eating bread and oil for over two thousand years before the tomato knocked at the kitchen door.

Tomato-mania probably hit hardest in Italy where they consume twice as much as in Spain, our *gazpacho* notwithstanding.

'The tomato made its appearance in Catalonia as an exotic novelty, rather like those we find on an expensive menu today: mango sorbet, reindeer steak or fillet of ostrich. Now that the ostrich has been acclimatized to our country, soon it'll no longer be a novelty, and that's what happened to the tomato,' explains Antoni Pinya.

We islanders, who are a breed unto ourselves, readily accept outside customs as long as it's the outsiders who practice them; it takes us a while longer to adopt them ourselves.

'In the eighteenth century, tomato was added to the basic bread & oil as an *esnobisme*, just as ham was twenty years ago, just as the thousand and one variants are being added to bread & oil today. In the Balearics we still differentiate between plain *pa amb oli* and *pa amb oli i tomàtiga*.[1] In Catalonia, on the other hand, *pa amb oli* turned into *pa amb tomàquet*[2] so rapidly that today, in many cases, they practically forget about the oil altogether.'

A couple of hundred years is all we needed to make the tomato very much our own. In the Balearics, depending on the village and on the context, *una tomàtiga* can also be taken to mean a common cold, a dim-witted girl or a state of legless drunkenness, apart from the predictably ribald references to the female anatomy. A couple of centuries has also given us time to make the acquaintance of other American members of the same botanical family, such as potatoes[3] and capsicum peppers, and acclimatize them not only to our agriculture but also to our diet, where they are usually combined with our own onions or garlic. It's strange to think that before the year 1700 nobody had tasted a *trempó* or a *tumbet*; nor a *gazpacho*, *ratatouille*, *pisto*, *sanfaina* or any other of the thousands of Mediterranean conjugations based on this family of vegetables. The aubergine or egg-plant, although botanically related, was introduced a lot earlier by the Arabs who brought it from central Asia.

In the Balearics we cultivate many kinds of tomatoes. Every year the farmers are offered the latest hybrid seeds, some of which don't even have a name, only a catalogue number, yet the time-tested traditional varieties still endure. The best known are the *tomàtiga de pruna* which is

---

[1] There are many regional variations; in the Balearics it's *tomàtiga* or *domàtiga*; in Catalonia, *tomàquet* or *tomaca*; in Valencia, *tomata*.

[2] Pronounced *too-mah-kit*, as in 'tomàquet, tomàquet, to buy a fat pig…'.

[3] The potato is Majorca's most important export, yet many older Majorcans still don't take it seriously, and consider it more of a garnish than a staple food.

small and round; and the *forastera* or 'outsider', an early tomato with pale flesh looking a bit flattened and creased as if somebody sat on it. The *mallorquina* is larger and ripens later than the *forastera*; the *valldemossina* is large and slightly elongated, fleshy and with few seeds; then, of course, there is the *murciana* which is the largest of all, a beefsteak tomato which is good for salads. The Majorcan farmers have also grown a lot of pear tomatoes—we also call them Swiss—for bottling whole or as sauce to keep through the winter.

Hanging tomatoes
(*Tomàtiga de Penjar*)

The kind of tomato that interests us most to rub on our bread & oil is commonly known as the *tomàtiga de penjar* or 'tomato for hanging up', although strictly speaking there is more than one variety that fits this description.[4] These tomatoes can be classified as autochthonous to the Balearics, although they are sporadically cultivated around Valencia where they're known as *tomacó*. A friend of mine reported seeing strings of tomatoes similar to ours in Liguria, Italy.

What's special about our hanging tomatoes is an anti-ageing gene which affects their chemical composition and allows them to keep fresh for months, simply strung up in a larder. The skin contains a natural inhibitor which prevents the seeds from germinating until the appropriate season. If you wash the tomato, this inhibitor is lost and the tomato follows suit. The size is also a longevity factor; the smaller the tomato, the greater the relation of skin to flesh, and the better it will keep.

---

[4] The hanging tomato is small, compact, with a tough skin and pasty flesh. The colour varies from dark pink to orange, although the irrigated varieties are redder, giving it the name *de ferro*.

Curiously enough, Israeli genetic engineers have introduced this Majorcan anti-ageing gene into a Canary Island salad tomato, creating a hybrid with an extended shelf-life. The patent was bought by a German company who sells the seeds to the hothouse agribusiness growers on the south-east coast of Spain, who in turn sell lorry-loads of these half-caste tomatoes to our hotels and markets, completing the circle.

There are two basic sub-varieties of hanging tomatoes. If the farmer intends to irrigate the plants, he will sow the variety known as *tomàtiga de ferro*, 'iron' or 'rust tomatoes'. If he has no water for irrigation and has to cultivate them as a dry-crop depending solely on rainfall, he will choose the variety known as *tomàtiga de ramellet*, 'little cluster tomatoes'. Today, most people erroneously identify all hanging tomatoes as *tomàtigues de ramellet*. Both these varieties have their local variants with descriptive names: *de burot* (scribbled), *de capoll curt* or *capoll llarg* (short or long stalk), *punxorada* (punctured)…

The *ferro* tomato plant, if it's well irrigated, can produce as many kilos of fruit as a salad tomato vine, and it is also grown on a cane trellis reinforced with oleaster poles. The harvest begins in July, but at that moment they can't compete in the market with the glut of the usual summer varieties, so they are placed on cane lattice trays or sewn onto strings over the hot months—a pleasant job in a cool patio—and begin to appear in the market in late September. In any case, people tend to associate the strings of hanging tomatoes with the arrival of autumn, and don't normally buy them until the cool weather begins. This is time to buy, at a cheaper price, the hanging tomatoes which have been rejected by the stringers as the wrong shape or size, or unlikely to keep well. A third of the crop of *tomàtiga de ferro* is set aside to be placed on the market after Christmas. Having been irrigated, the plants produce larger tomatoes than those cultivated as a dry-crop but being less hardy, they only keep until about February.

The real *tomàtiga de ramellet* keeps all winter and is still fit to eat in May when the new season's salad tomatoes appear. In Majorca it is grown mainly in the village of Sant Joan and the six parishes that surround it—cereal and melon country—as well as in the dry parts of Minorca and Ibiza. It's the only variety that will thrive in these arid conditions.

The *ramellet* plant isn't guided up trellises, it's allowed to grow sprawling along the ground and is often planted between rows of melons, (another ground-hugging dry-crop) because the times for planting, hoeing and harvesting coincide. If it doesn't rain, the tomato crop is small; if it rains too much, or at the wrong time, it's lost. When the fruit begins to turn colour, the skin loses its elasticity; if a late downpour causes it to grow more, the skin splits.

These tomatoes grow on little sprigs, *ramellets*, of five tomatoes each; the name refers to these sprigs and not, as most people wrongly assume, to the finished strings of tomatoes for sale. The whole sprig can be picked as soon as the last tomato is ripe, and most families used to hang them from nails in the roof-beams or on a wire stretched across the open attic, to save the time and bother of stringing them. Today, however, nearly all the production is sewn onto strings, because they fetch a much higher price this way.

The *ramellet* crop begins in mid-August. Only a third is put on the market before Christmas; the rest takes up the slack as stocks of the *ferro* variety begin to dry up around February. Strings of *tomàtigues de ramellet* can still be found in the market at the end of May.

Why are hanging tomatoes even more expensive than the out-of-season greenhouse tomatoes you find in the market? It's not only the extra work of stringing them; it simply doesn't lend itself to intensive farming and mass-marketing. The cultivation, collecting and stringing is done on a family basis. The picking has to be done by hand, the plant being visited several times in order to pluck the tomatoes at the right moment of ripeness. Supermarket toms are picked green and turn colour on the way to market, but the hanging tomatoes have to ripen under the sun, absorbing its full power. The advantage is evident when you compare the nutritive values of a *tomàtiga de ramellet* (seven months after picking) with a fresh salad tomato (a couple of days after picking). Even with the same proportion of water, the hanging tomato has a much higher concentration of minerals; for every gram of pulp, it has fifty per cent more protein, calcium and sodium, double the quantity of iron and triple the amount of potassium, and yet only half the carbons and calories. And we haven't even mentioned the flavour! Whether scrubbed on your bread & oil or used for cooking, a little goes a lot further than a greenhouse tomato.

All autochthonous varieties or breeds, whether animal (the Majorcan donkey or the black pig) or vegetable, (the hanging tomato, the light green pepper, the sweet white onion and purple carrot), are perfectly adapted to the climate and soil of our islands, and so hardly need any of the special treatments required by imported hybrids or cross-breeds. Our vegetables are quite happy without hothouses, chemical fertilizers and pesticides. They thrive with organic farming techniques, which are basically our grandparents' methods updated; you can find strings of 'ecological' tomatoes in health shops and market stalls, or directly from organic farms such as Sa Teulera near Manacor. Yet you're pretty safe buying traditional varieties of local vegetables from any market stall that sells its own produce; few small-scale farms bother to spend money on chemicals when they can perfectly well get a good, unblemished crop without.

After Christmas, the price of the *enfilalls* (strings of tomatoes) creeps up because they have lost some weight, and the blemished or rotten tomatoes have to be weeded out. Normally one buys a whole *enfilall* but the price goes by weight; thus, it's not considered bad form for a customer to pick off any tomato he doesn't like the look of before the *enfilall* goes on the scales.

To *enfilar* is simple but requires a lot of practice before reaching the speed of fifteen kilos an hour. The strings are usually 40 cm long (holding about 2.5 kilos) or 80 cm (5 kg). The process begins by sitting oneself comfortably on a chair before a tripod about a metre and a half high with a hook in the centre from which the string, made of pita fibre or synthetic raffia, is hanging from a looped knot. The fruit should have been picked with the short stem intact; the needle is pushed through it and the thread pulled tightly, fastening the tomato to the string. The tomatoes must keep clear of one another; if they touch, there's a danger of rot or mould setting in. A nice compact *enfilall* may look more attractive but it won't keep as long.

The hanging tomato grows well where other varieties can't, even in the coastal areas, because the sea breeze doesn't harm it. The tomato is one of the few plants which withstand saline conditions; Banyalbufar was famous all over the island for its tomato production, grown on the terraces overlooking the sea. On the south coast of Spain, I've seen tomatoes grown on the beach.

Sun-dried tomatoes

In humid areas like the Sóller valley, where there's an excellent irrigation system set up by the Arabs in the tenth century, there was no need to depend upon dry-crop hanging tomatoes. The custom there has always been to grow pear tomatoes for bottling, and other varieties for sun-drying as they do in parts of Italy.

According to Cati of the *Cals Vinagrers* stall in the town's market, 'they used to do a lot of tomato drying here in Sóller, there was always plenty of water and the plants would produce quantities of tomatoes, big ones, but only in the summer; in the winter there'd be no fresh tomatoes. On the plain, the *tomàtiga de ramellet* grows better, it's a dry crop, but not here, there was probably too much water and all! Now some of the Sóller farmers have begun to grow hanging tomatoes, but that's because it doesn't rain as much as it used to and there's not such a risk of them spoiling. On the other side of the island they hardly knew what a dried tomato was, but here we used it for cooking, for making *sopes*, it's a concentrated tomato.'

The technique consists in cutting the tomato in two horizontally, salting it and laying it out on cane trays in the sun. 'The process is simple but it needs a lot of care and attention, you have to cover the tomatoes or bring them under cover when the *serena* (the evening dew) falls because it will leave them damp and interrupt the drying process, spoiling them. There's nothing to it but salt and sun. Once dried, you can put them in a jar with a bit of oil, but that's not really necessary. I make a whole lot every summer, we love to eat it with our *pa amb oli…* it's better than a slice of *serrano* ham.'

And one of Cati's clients, an American woman who has spent nearly fifty years on the island, remarks: 'These dried tomatoes are almost fermented. That's what gives them that special taste, it transcends the taste of tomato. The salt ferments the tomato as it cures in the sun, rather like the oriental pickles—miso paste, for instance, which is soya fermented with salt—or like sauerkraut.'

The most common way of preserving tomato in the Mediterranean is to bottle it whole or as sauce, which we call *tomatigat*. Here's how they used to do it in the *possessió* of Son Marroig: 'We clean the tomatoes, better if they're *de pruna* or *de carabasseta*, and put them in glass jars with a spoonful of salt and another of sugar, then top up with water. Then we seal the jars with the corking machine and put them in the bread oven when we've taken the bread out. We leave them there until the oven has completely cooled down.'

Another method, for those who don't have a bread oven handy, is to heat the sealed jars in the bain-marie (double saucepan method), but they shouldn't be taken out of the water until it has returned to room temperature, or the jars may crack.

Chapter 7

Bread & oil &————?

The headmistress of our local primary school has had to help children of many nationalities adapt to our local language and customs.

'To be able to assimilate another culture, it is important to first know your own: who you are and where you come from.'

In the case of *pa amb oli*, we now know what it is and where it comes from, but what company does it keep? Should it adapt itself to foreign influences, or incorporate them into its own character?

'Bread & oil has the great advantage,' says Antoni Pinya, 'of combining well with almost any food, be it animal or vegetable. It doesn't clash with anything except perhaps other fats; you wouldn't want to eat it with *sobrassada* or with oleaginous fruits such as hazelnuts. At least, that doesn't square with our way of thinking. But certainly eat it with raisins, dried figs, a slice of apple or orange, all kinds of vinegar pickles, cheeses and cold cooked or cured meats. Dried fish also used to be a popular accompaniment: herring, cod, *capellans*,[1] or *calamar*. The trouble with

---

[1] 'Chaplains', a small hake.

fish is that your fingers absorb the volatile oils and you smell of herring for the rest of the day. In the old days you'd eat a *pa amb oli* with spring garlic which was a joy, but that's also incompatible with today's social relations. Before getting your teeth into a *pa amb oli* with garlic or dried herring, you have to stop and think, "Wait a minute, this afternoon I've got to go and see so-and-so…," and that's why the habit has all but disappeared.'

'We're always on the look out for something to go with our bread & oil. There's always been a very clear idea of what a *berenada*[2] should be: bread & oil AND…'

The *pa amb oli* culture undergoes local variations. In Sóller, for instance, it used to be commonly eaten with lightly-salted cod or with fresh orange slices. This would probably surprise a farmer from the centre of the island whose bread & oil was usually accompanied by some pork sausage or dried fruits. These little idiosyncrasies, such as whether to apply the oil before or after the salt or the tomato, have made of the *pa amb oli* a dynamic, living culture, with local, tribal and even individual variants.

'A *pa amb oli* is simply bread and olive oil. That said, I don't think there's anything that you couldn't eat with it, whatever takes your fancy,' states Tomeu Torrens. 'I know loads of youngsters who dunk their *pa amb oli amb tomàtiga* into a glass of chocolate milk, even in their *cafè amb llet*, I've seen them do it. What we can't do is change our bread & oil's basic identity. We have to know what it is, but from that point on, everybody's quite free to eat it the way they want and with whatever they feel like. The more variety

---

[2] A *berenada* is a slap-up *berenar*. And a *berenar* is an all-purpose term for anything eaten between main meals; it applies to breakfast, elevenses, afternoon tea, mid-morning or mid-afternoon snack, the munchies or a night-cap. A *berenada* is more on the scale of a brunch or a high tea.

you surround it with, the more it makes your mouth water.

'Take a slice of bread & oil with some sweet green pepper and a couple of split olives. They're all cold, unprocessed foods. You take these four ingredients, and you've got a full meal. That's all you need, but you can add anything you like.'

Garlic

Until that plump, blushing American upstart the tomato elbowed her way in, the favourite companion to a *pa amb oli* used to be the headstrong, fiery Mediterranean garlic. Scrubbed onto bread before adding the oil, garlic will give it an unbeatable fragrance and charisma. To get the most out of your clove of garlic, slice off the hard bit at the bottom and start scrubbing the clove across the grain. The bread has to act as sandpaper, so it should be consistent and, if possible, toasted, otherwise you can only scrub along the crust.

'Garlic is one of the pillars of Majorcan cooking, but it should be eaten raw to get the most of its natural antibiotic properties; as they say, *all cuinat, all perdut*: garlic cooked, garlic lost. Like all natural medicines, it's more preventative than curative. Some raw garlic daily will keep your defences on their toes. It's better to prevent with your diet than cure with medicines, because medical treatment is like the fire brigade: it'll put out the fire but leave the house a complete mess.'

We Mediterraneans have turned our backs on raw garlic wherever tourism has taken hold; this is due mainly to the attitude of the north Europeans. If a northerner wants to put down a Spaniard, an Italian, a Greek or even a Frenchman, you can bet that the insult will include some reference to the stink of garlic.

The similarity of pronunciation between *alls* (garlic in the plural) and the English 'ice' has led to much confusion. When Sebastià the fisherman took over our village bar, one of his first foreign customers complained that her Coca-Cola was warm. She pointed at the glass and demanded 'Ice!' Sebastià raised his eyebrows, took the glass and came back with a couple of heads of garlic floating in the warm Coke.

When in season, tender garlic shoots are delicious with bread & oil; local variations include spring onions and, around Sa Pobla, spring leeks (no pun intended). There is also a hedgerow variety of wild garlic which in late autumn produces edible white bell-shaped flowers. The chive-like stems, triangular in cross-section, are also delicious.

Olives

A *pa amb oli brut*[3] is the most primitive form of bread & oil, 'a slice of bread toasted on the embers and rubbed with *pansida*[4] olives', according to the Alcover dictionary. 'That's the truth', swears Pere, a friend from Fornalutx. 'During the famine, when there was no oil, my grandparents would sometimes rub windfall olives onto a crust of bread.'

Olives are the perfect complement to a *pa amb oli*, although an outsider might consider it a superfluity to eat olives with oil.

'Many things go well alongside bread & oil; vinegar pickles, hot peppers, raw vegetables… but never forget some olives!' says Toni Mateu, managing director of *Olives Caimari*. 'We began to prepare olives commercially thirty-

---

[3] Dirty *pa amb oli*.

[4] Literally, shrivelled (meaning dried, as a raisin or prune). They can be eaten raw.

five years ago, but it was a failure because the women in the villages all used to prepare their own. Now they sell very well because young women today prefer to buy them ready to eat; they no longer have the time or the know-how to do it themselves.'

If you don't grow olives yourself, you can buy them in the markets in October and November, and preparing them is a lot easier than many people imagine. If your parents never taught you how, you'll find the technique in the recipe section of this book.

In Majorca and Ibiza there are several different ways of preparing them, according to the type of olive: *pansida* or *cendrosa* (cindery) brown olives; green, either split (*trencada*) or whole (*sencera*); black (*negra*) or blue (*blava*). These are all the same variety of olive, the *mallorquina*, in different stages of ripeness. In Minorca, where the almost constant wind makes olive cultivation impossible, the peasants salt the tiny *olivó*, the fruit of the oleaster.

Pa torrat	Toasted bread
oli novell	Just-pressed oil
olives cendroses	Cindery olives
d'aquí al cel!	and straight to heaven!

recites Pere Colom, a young poet and farmer. 'The first windfalls, from the trees that get the most sun, are those that have ripened before time. The little oil they give is very acid, so that's why they're gathered from the ground around October, to get them out of the way before the black ones fall. You can eat them almost immediately, because they have lost their astringency; they just need dressing with oil, salt, lemon juice and laurel leaves. These bluish-coloured olives are wrinkled, which is why they're known as *pansides*. But among the *pansides* you also find another kind which you can distinguish by their brown colour and by a certain dustiness, like a mantle of cinders, which gives them the name *cendroses*. The farmers who know a thing or two about olives pick them out and prepare them separately because they consider them finer and tastier.'

It takes a practised eye to select the *pansides* from other unripe windfalls which can't be eaten raw.

'When my aunt gathers *pansides*, every one is a winner,' says Francesca Deyá. 'But we can all tell when my mother has been picking them because we have to spit one out every so often. Of course, she's from the plain and didn't marry into an olive-picking family until she was nineteen.'

'In the old days' continues Pere, 'nobody would eat a whole olive in one mouthful, they'd nibble at them to make them last longer. The olives they had put in brine had to last until the following autumn. And even if you had plenty in the larder, in my grandparents' time it was bad manners to eat an olive at one go… it goes to show how times have changed. Today people eat them two or three at a time!'

'There's one truth as big as a temple,' says Toni Mateu, 'and that is that our local products, especially fruit and vegetables, are often a lot better than those we import. People should think about it: in terms of value for money, it's best to buy local produce, as long as our budgets allow it. The Majorcan olives that we pickle in brine cost us twice as much as imported ones of similar characteristics, and that's due to the cost of picking them by hand, and yet people buy them. Now, a split green olive from the mainland comes out all right, but it's not quite the same; the Majorcan olive has a finer pulp. As for the Majorcan *pansida*, there's no other variety of olive from the Peninsula that matches it if you want to prepare it in the traditional way. The *pansida* season is short; we don't bottle them, we simply dress them and they're sold through the market stalls by weight. They're quick to fix with a few cloves of garlic, a bay leaf, some drops of oil, a pinch of salt and the whole lot stirred about in an earthenware *greixionera*... this kind of olive is delicious.

'The best kind of olive to my mind is the green Majorcan *trencada* (split) olive, with that touch of fennel and lemon leaf... if you know how, you can have it ready to eat in two weeks. The *sencera* or whole green olive needs to have a whole twelve months run over it because it's harder to "kill",[5] it's best after spending a year in brine. The mainland olives are softened and "killed" with soda, they're "cooked up" as we say. But the Majorcan olive has to die at the hands of time, with only the help of salt and water. Here on the island, we prepare all our olives naturally. All those *manzanilla* and those anchovy-flavoured olives, they're all cooked with soda; not that there's anything wrong with it, it's just a way of speeding up the process. But we've never done that here.'

As for the *oliva negra* or *blava*, very little is prepared commercially; they are the last Majorcan olives to ripen and don't warrant a special trip to the oil press, so they are set aside and put in brine. 'The black Aragonese olives that are cultivated on the island are really good for eating; it's a sin, once you start eating them you can't stop. The queen of the black olives, however, is the *pansida mallorquina*.'

---

[5] Dead, or slaked, means that the olive has lost its natural astringency, the effect of making your mouth pucker. The *pansides* have lost their astringency naturally, but otherwise this is done by soaking in brine, or industrially in a soda solution.

The world of olives knows no bounds and it's worth while investigating all the varieties you possibly can, although we islanders, when we buy olives at the market stalls, tend to choose local produce. The dozens of different types which you can find there are no more than a tiny sample of the scores of varieties of Spanish olives and the many ways of preparing them, from the little *arbequina* to the giant Seville olive stuffed with a hot green pepper. In any Moroccan market you'll find as many varieties again, most of which you've probably never seen before; not to mention hundreds more in Italy, France, Turkey, Greece, Tunisia, Cyprus or Lebanon.

Envinagrats or vinegar pickles

Civilization has always used five basic substances to preserve food, because they are hostile to bacteria and yet tolerable, or even appetizing, to humans: salt, sugar, fats (oil or lard), vinegar and alcohol. Neither sugar nor alcohol are as important in these latitudes as they are to those living in colder climates, where the calories obtained from jams and fruit bottled in syrup or brandy help to fend off the cold. The northerner's sweet tooth is evident even in their vinegar pickles; compare a Hayward's pickled onion or a Kuhne gherkin with our local equivalent such as Roselló, Caimari or other Majorcan brands.

'We prepare and bottle our *envinagrats* with the Majorcan palate in mind,' explains a *vinagrer* who runs a pickling plant on the industrial estate east of Palma. 'The foreigners find them a bit sharp, so we also distribute a German brand to the local shops because the Teutonic residents are after their own products, which I think is perfectly normal. As for our own people, I'd recommend that they buy local brands because today the shops here are flooded with stuff from outside. We now put a little silhouette of the island on the label so that it's immediately recognizable as a Balearic product. Our authorities prattle on about supporting everything local, but it's mainly hot air. Our products face some heavy competition because the whole world wants to sell their wares here. As for exports, all I can say is that our star product is easy to take away with you: a good suntan.'

The vinegar pickles we most commonly associate with our bread & oil are obviously *fonoll marí* (pickled samphire) and *pebres coents* (hot green peppers). Other favourites are *taperes* (capers, the unopened bud of the caper plant), *cavalls* (the fruit of the same plant, which looks like a gooseberry with a stalk at each end) and the *envinagrat* (a mixture of pearl onions, gherkins, carrots and cauliflower in vinegar).

Samphire or sea-fennel is a perennial plant with aromatic, fleshy leaves, whose natural habitat is the rocky seashore, from the southern coasts of the British Isles to the Black Sea. It grows especially well on sunny cliff-faces, seemingly out of reach of all but the goats. There's a reference in Shakespeare's King Lear: 'Half-way down hangs one that gathers samphire, dreadful trade.' It's an example of how far our ancestors would venture in order to vary and enrich their diet. In the rest of Europe, samphire is all but ignored; in some places it is occasionally eaten as a boiled vegetable. We Mediterraneans soak it in brine before steeping it in vinegar; the British would boil it between the brine and the vinegar, perhaps because their samphire isn't as tender as ours. The most renowned pickled samphire on the island, which we would eat at home whenever we got the chance, is prepared by the hermits of the Ermita de la Trinitat. These bearded hermits know exactly where the best samphire and wild caper plants grow along the Valldemossa sea-cliffs, as well as the best moment for picking them. You'll find more about samphire and capers in the recipe chapter.

You can buy bottled capers, samphire, hot peppers and *vinagrats* in most village shops or supermarkets, or by weight in those market stalls or shops which sell olives, dried fish, and cooked pulses such as chickpeas and beans.

As for the benefits and perils of vinegar, there's a wide range of opinions; on the one hand, it stimulates the flow of gastric juices, thus aiding digestion, but in excess it can affect the count of red and white corpuscles in the blood.

Here in the Mediterranean, we always associate vinegar with the grape; after all, *vinagre* means sour wine. But outside the wine belt people have turned to other sources, such as malt which produces a more full-bodied vinegar, and cider, which reputedly makes for the healthiest of all, and is the kind served in vegetarian restaurants. On the islands we don't flavour our vinegars like the French or age them like the Italians; we might have a lot to learn, but when we like something as it is, why mess about with it?

Crudités

Thanks to our climate, tempered by the sea, we're lucky enough to have fresh vegetables on hand all year round which we can eat raw with our *sopes*, with an *arròs brut* or a *pa amb oli*. Even in January, there's always a spring onion or garlic, carrots or radishes, not to mention lettuces. Our sweet white onion and autochthonous green pepper, with its light green skin and thick flesh, are virtually unknown on the mainland; neither should ever be absent from a good *trempó* salad, but they are equally at home on a plate of bread & oil, along with some slices of giant Majorcan radish. Raw vegetables and fruit help the body in three ways: by providing fibre for the digestive system, a full set of vitamins and minerals for the organism and a crispness to help maintain healthy teeth and gums. (However, dentists working here point out that the bad state of most of our gnashers by no means reflects a diet of raw veg and crisp toast!)

There are good alimentary reasons for starting a meal with a bite of salad, fruit or raw vegetables. Let's not forget that we are biologically programmed to eat raw food; three or four millennia of cooking is a wink of an eye in human history. Yet in spite of the enormous variety of foods available, we have a very limited repertoire compared with our hunter–gatherer ancestors who would have tasted hundreds of different edible plants, fruits, roots, seeds, grains, flowers, fungi, insects and animals in their short lives. Cooking, of course has allowed us access to otherwise inedible grains and plants. We are culturally (if not biologically) so adapted to cooked food that many of us would need enormous willpower to return to absolute crudivorism.

Even though we may be totally adapted to cooked food, having been brought up on Granny's *fava parada*, our digestive system responds more favourably and handles heavy foods better if we whet our appetite beforehand with some radishes, olives or salad. It's like leaving the choke open a while before letting out the clutch.

A complete *pa amb oli* is mostly uncooked; cold-pressed olive oil, tomatoes, salt, garlic; also the vegetables or fruit and the vinegar pickles. Let's not forget the *serrano* ham, the cheese or the anchovies, all of which are cured but not cooked. The bread, of course is; but, if made in the traditional way, it undergoes a natural process with a result less taxing to our gastric department than ready-sliced sandwich bread.

Most of us place our ham, cheese, anchovies or whatever, on the slice of bread, but not raw vegetables, fruit, olives or pickles. It feels more natural to alternate bites, holding the slice of bread in one hand and the complement in the other. This is specially true when it's long and thin—carrot, celery, fresh green or hot pickled pepper or spring onion.

A more refined approach is of course to prepare the *crudités* beforehand and arrange them on your slices of *pa amb oli*, leaving your left hand free to manage the wineglass, but you risk losing the spontaneity of 'now a bit of this, now a bit of that.' The Italians often eat their *bruschetta* with slices of raw mushroom on it; I've found that snow peas (raw or lightly sautéed to bring out the colour and reduce squeakiness) are perfect astride a slice of bread & oil.

Any raw vegetables that look tired after a day or two in the shop or the fridge—snow peas, lettuce, radishes, carrots —can recuperate their terseness and crispness after a warm bath: ten minutes in warm water then ten more in cold should do it.

The woman who farms a couple of terraces near my orchard noticed that someone had been eating her tender new fava beans, and that the culprit had tossed the empty husks to the ground. Her suspicions immediately fell upon a couple of Andalucian labourers who had been working nearby. 'It must have been an outsider,' she fumed, 'no Majorcan would eat a raw fava!' Some time later, in a Spanish gypsy cookery book, I found the following recipe: 'Take a hunk of bread and hollow out the crumb, pour in some olive oil and fill it with peeled tender fava beans. Eat it accompanied with dried cod.' (This lightly salted, chewy cod is sold ready-to-eat in polythene bags in the market.)

'En Molinet', a professional cook from Sant Llorenç tells me how he prepares fresh white Majorcan onion to eat with bread & oil: 'Slice it vertically into thin new-moons, leave it for a couple of days with salt and vinegar in a glass jar, then eat it raw with your bread & oil. That's the way they do it in Valencia. The way we prepare spring onion around Manacor, is to first top-and-tail it and take off the tough skin. With a sharp knife we make two crossed cuts at the base so that it splays out in four prongs, then we put some oil, salt and vinegar on a saucer and use the onion to stir the dressing. Take a bite, stir some more, take another, till you get to the green part.'

The dried tomato can almost be considered a raw vegetable but the taste is so concentrated that in *pa amb oli* culture it falls into the same category as ham, fish or cheese.

Fresh Herbs

Aromatic herbs open up your bread & oil to a whole new register of flavours, aromas and textures. We can use them to flavour our olive oil (see the recipe section) or eat them fresh. Try your bread and oil with a sprig of basil or a sprinkling of chopped oregano, thyme, sage, parsley, coriander, marjoram or fennel. Even if you don't have a herb garden, a window box will do; most herbs are hardier than flowers, and there are two stalls in Palma's Olivar market, by the Plaça Roselló entrance, which always have potted herbs available for transplanting. The hypermarkets now sell fresh herbs too, in pots or freshly cut and packaged in cellophane, although the fluorescent lighting intended to make them appear more appetizing often has the opposite effect.

In some parts of the island where the farmland is irrigated, such as Manacor or Andratx, a popular herb to eat with your bread & oil is *verdolaga* (*Portulaca oleracea*), a kind of cress that trails beside the irrigation ditches and in the vegetable plots. It has succulent little heart-shaped leaves with a neutral taste, like a lettuce leaf. It is used in *trempó* salad, but mainly alongside a *pa amb oli*.

For those who like strong tastes, there are always the peppery nasturtium flowers or the wild garlic mentioned earlier. Tender wild asparagus shoots, although not strictly a herb, are also a seasonal delight alongside your *pa amb oli*, eaten raw or simply sautéed for a minute. Another hard-to-classify accompaniment, introduced by the foreigners and health-seeking urbanites and available year-round, is sprouts. A sprinkling of alfalfa sprouts on your bread & oil gives it a crisp freshness. The custom of eating germinated seeds is Oriental, but it forms an important part of a normal vegetarian diet. The amino acids, minerals and vitamins concentrated in the seed are easily assimilated when it germinates; this is the best way of capturing the vital energy it contains. A local company run by a British couple produces ready-sprouted green soya (mung bean), alfalfa or cress sprouts in bags available in health food stores and supermarkets. You can also do-it-yourself in a plastic germinator or simply on a polystyrene tray under a damp cloth, at a constant temperature of 18°C, rinsing them twice a day. Alfalfa and mung beans are the most popular but you can successfully germinate lentils, chick peas or wheat.

Cheese

'All cheeses are good with bread & oil. There are no two that taste the same. This one is tender, that one is stronger, one tastes of the cow and another of the barrel.'

Uncured or fresh cheeses go well with stronger accompaniments to your bread & oil, such as olives and vinegar pickles. Stronger, cured varieties combine and contrast well with sweeter companions like Muscat grapes or, as is the custom in Minorca, with apple and pumpkin jam, in a combination known as *jaleo*.

'At home we'd always eat fresh sheep's cheese with plain bread and oil; we'd leave off the tomato because it would give it that little bit of acidity that seems to kill the taste of the cheese.'

Many of the traditions and habits of our country kitchens which are followed today for the sheer gastronomic pleasure they produce, prove on closer inspection to be simply ways of making unpalatable food fit for the table. Fried *sobrassada* with honey and sweet wine is an example; today it is served in the best restaurants, but it originated as a way of getting the family to eat the last dry, gritty *sobrassades* of the season.

Another example is cheese steeped in olive oil:

'When someone had an open cheese that had begun to dry out, they'd chop it up into cubes and stick it in a glass jar topped up with olive oil and then eat it with their *pa amb oli*. Now it's sold as a very expensive delicatessen product, in an arty jar with a little wooden spoon or fork.

'In Majorca we used to eat our home-made cheese fresh, it wasn't everybody who had a chance to eat it cured. We even used to use bread crumbs on our macaroni. Very few people knew how to cure cheese, or had the moulds with which to form the pieces. The technique was to salt it, rub it with oil and paprika which formed a protective layer, and leave it to cure, turning the piece over every day so that it wouldn't get damp.'

In terms of daily fat intake, the Minorcans have

substituted their lack of local olive oil with dairy products. Several factors have contributed to the importance of dairy farms on the island: the cooler, less humid climate, the British cultural heritage dating from the 1708 occupation, the system of universal heir that kept large, profitable farms intact. Majorca and Ibiza's dairy produce was based mainly on goat or sheep's milk, or mixture of both, like the exquisite cheese now being made by s'Atalaia in Llucmajor. Majorcan cow cheese is normally sold fresh, 'creamy' or semi-cured; our humidity doesn't allow the pieces to mature as well as in windswept Minorca.

'Before the tourists began to arrive in Majorca, cow's cheese was only being made in the Levant of the island, around Artà. The pieces were small and very tanned, but it was very tasty, and since we had nothing else, it went down really well!

'The proper traditional Mahon farmhouse cheese from Minorca is only made in the wintertime; it's kept in a cellar or a drying shed where it matures and ages to the point where, if we want to cut it with a knife, it crumbles. Once a cheese is open, it won't mature any more.

'The *formatge maonès* was the first imported cheese we ever tasted, and here we learned to eat it with fruit. As the pieces age, so the different fruits ripen; in April the *nispros*[6], then the June apricots, the St James grapes followed by the August grapes, then the figs… every time we open a new cheese, it seems that its point of maturity perfectly complements whichever fruit is in season. The sharper spring fruits go well with a mild cheese, while the sweeter summer and autumn fruits—including dried apricots, prunes or raisins—offset the bite of a mature cheese.'

---

[6] Loquats.

Eggs

A supper of bread & oil with omelette or scrambled eggs is a traditional way to end the working day, and kids love it. They also love bread & oil soldier-boys dipped in soft-boiled or fried egg. A very common supper in the convents and monasteries of old Castile consisted of slices of toast, rubbed with raw garlic and dipped in an olive-oil *vinagreta*, then covered with alternating slices of hard-boiled egg and salad tomato and eaten accompanied with black olives. A variant introduced by my teenage daughter consists of using slices of Chinese-style pickled eggs (hard boiled eggs left a month in spiced vinegar).

Another way of serving up eggs with bread & oil, which can only come from such a culturally eclectic kitchen as my own, is to lightly oil-and-tomato a slice of stale bread, soak it in beaten egg and then fry it to make eggy bread & oil, a.k.a. French-Majorcan Toast.

Embotits:[7] the cold table

The cold meats in the Balearics are very varied, but virtually all are pork-based. It's ironic then, that most people who eat bread & oil in a bar will order it with cured ham, precisely the one pork product that has never been made here on the islands. It is no less ironic that our most popular export to the mainland, *sobrassada*, is hardly ever seen in the company of a *pa amb oli*. Of course, unlike the lean *serrano*, *jabugo* and *iberico* pigs, our Majorcan black breed carried a lot of fat, putting our local pork products (especially the *sobrassada* whose ingredients are uncooked) at odds with oily bread. But there's another reason for the incompatibility:

---

[7] The word *embotit*, from the verb meaning 'to stuff or to cram' refers mainly to pork sausages of various types—from *chorizo* or *salami* to *sobrassada* or haggis-like *morcilla* and, by extension, any cold meats, patés, etc.

'I think the main reason they don't marry well, is that we like to enjoy the full taste of a well-cured *sobrassada*, with plain Majorcan bread,' explains the owner of one of Palma's best groceries, near the Town Hall. 'If you add oil, you can't appreciate the full flavour of either. If I lived in a colder climate and needed more calories, I'd probably eat my *sobrassada* with bread and butter instead. I've had Catalan customers who take home one of our black pig *sobrassades* and to eat with their *pa amb tomàquet*, even though they use a very strong-tasting *arbequina* olive oil. But our custom is to keep them separate.'

With the *sobrassada* taken care of, and leaving the *jamón serrano* aside for the time being, what other *embotits* do we have? In Majorca, the most popular is the *camaiot* and *varia negre*, both consisting of the same ingredients but stuffed into different parts of the pig's anatomy. The stuffing is made of all the edible parts that are left over from the pig once the *sobrassada*, the *botifarra* and *botifarrons* are made. These last two are blood sausages and are best eaten within a week of being made, roasted over the embers and eaten with bread. The *camaiot*, being stuffed into a thicker skin, lasts longer and can be cut into thin slices to lay on your bread & oil.

'We have our *sobrassada*, the Minorcans their *carn i xuia* ("lean and bacon") which is a kind of salami but with a very different bouquet. For some reason, it goes very well with our *pa amb oli*, the combination is exquisite. It's not just recently that you can find it on this island; I can remember eating it here forty years ago, but we hadn't generally cottoned on to it then like we have now. Every week more than twenty kilos of hand-made *carn i xuia* leave Son Vivot, our shop here in the Porta Pintada, just off the Plaça d'Espanya, in Palma.'

The traditional pork products made by hand or on a small scale, on the brink of economic extinction only five years ago, are now making a big comeback. If the return to organic meats in the north of Europe is an ethical reaction to the treatment of battery farm animals and the food scandals, in our part of the world it's more of a question of taste and health:

'The *embotits* we sell in Son Vivot are made by craftsmen, we pay the farmers extra so they can breed the pigs without animal feed; instead they fatten them the traditional way with fava beans, figs, and acorns… that way you get a well fattened pig of excellent quality. Six years ago the local breed of black pig was brought back from the point of extinction; it has more fat so we mix the meat with some from a normal pig. The *sobrassada* is made with paprika from Pòrtol, which is more expensive but better quality than the stuff they bring over from the mainland. We also have *camaiot, varia negre, botifarró, blanquet*, all made in the traditional manner.'

Here we ought to mention the case of Mateu 'Putxer' Torrens, of Sa Pobla, who has almost single-handedly raised our traditional pork products to a gourmet standard, investigating and rescuing recipes from centuries back, as well as experimenting with new combinations.

'The way a cured meat is sliced makes a difference to the taste,' remarks Xisca Soler, of the Bar Es Pa Amb Oliet in Deià; 'the knife must be well sharpened before you start, and your slices have to be as thin as possible, almost like wood shavings, so that the ham or the sausage releases all the flavour it contains. This makes even more sense when you're slicing from a leg of *jabugo* ham that cost you fifty thousand pesetas. Once I was interviewed for the job of maître at a good restaurant, and they asked me if I knew how to slice ham. I replied, 'If I can cover one of your plates'—about ten inches across—'with less than 100 grams of sliced ham, will you give me the job?' I did it with 98 grams and I was maître there for twelve years.

'A connoisseur will never ask you for *tacos*[8] of ham; cubes of cheese maybe, but the *tacos* are simply a way of making the most of the tail end of the ham, the part that you can't cut into slivers.'

Any Majorcan nationalist who wants to taste our equivalent to the proper cured *jamón serrano*, *de jabugo* or *iberico* should taste the cured pork made at Can Rafel in Artà. 'It's the closest local equivalent to *jamón serrano*. My grandparents used to make it at home, it's a way of keeping the best part of the pork loin which otherwise would have to be eaten fresh as steaks. They would soak the loin in brine, as if they were preparing olives. After forty-eight hours it would be taken out and left to cure in the open attic. We rub it with paprika and hang it up to dry in a stocking so that it "breathes" properly as it cures. After a couple of months, this here is what you get. There are very few people who make it to sell. It's expensive, but I find it as good as an *iberico* ham for which they're likely to charge you double.'

'First, cut a thick slice and take off the skin, then you can lay it on a cutting board and slice it vertically as thin as you like. That, on top of a *pa amb oli* made with hanging tomato, I'd rate as ten out of ten.'

Fish

'The way it was done in the old days was to scatter flakes of toasted herring on top of your bread & oil, a few olives on the side... oooooh! Now that's what I call a really

---

[8] Cubes of ham or cheese often served as *tapas* in the south of Spain.

Majorcan *pa amb oli*. Nobody eats that anymore, not because it isn't delicious but because they don't want to smell of fish.'

On the islands, inland communications were so bad until a couple of generations ago, that fresh fish was only eaten near the coast; none but the largest towns would have a fish market. Most of the fish consumed inland was either salted, marinated or, from the 1950s onwards, in cans.

A tuna fish *pa amb oli* is by now a classic, as is the canned sardine variation; today you can buy sardines with the skin and spine removed. But to know what's really good, you should try it with fried fresh baby sardines, like my wife makes. Ask the fishwife to clean and open them like a book, dust them in salt and flour, fry them quickly in very hot olive oil and eat them on a toasted bread & oil. Later on I'll talk about how to prepare *jarret* and marinated anchovies.

Most of the readers of this book are probably too young to know what to do with the dried salted herrings you can still see sold in village shops, laid out like the golden spokes of a wheel, in circular wooden trays. Toni Morlà, excellent songwriter and chronicler of our culture, explains the procedure: 'You wrap the herring in a piece of *paper d'estrassa* (rough sugar-paper), place it in the door-jamb and slam the door. The skin and the spine stay stuck to the paper, leaving the edible part ready to eat with your bread & oil. It helps to add a few drops of vinegar.'

At the other end of the scale, at the more sophisticated *pa amb oli* joints on the island, you can order yours with smoked salmon or caviar. At the home of a Swedish friend of ours, I found bread & oil with roll mop herrings to be delicious. You can find them in little glass jars in the cold section of your supermarket, where you'll also find tins of German-style filleted herring. If we're going to be culturally and gastronomically colonized by the Northern Barbarians, we might as well make the most of it!

Fresh Fruit

There are many varieties of fruit, vegetables and cereals that have gradually disappeared from our farmland, varieties that people appreciated for their special characteristics. Every one had its own peculiarity or attribute. Some were to be eaten immediately, others were for keeping, some to eat raw and others cooked. There were early and late varieties, to guarantee a continued supply of fresh produce, but most have disappeared under the avalanche of high-yield green-house produce.

One habit that seems to have died out with them is that of eating fruit with bread & oil. I know a lot of people who still eat theirs with June or September figs, grapes, slices of orange, pear or apple.

The custom of eating fruit and cheese is common to many cultures; as far as I've found out (which isn't very far), to eat it with bread & oil is peculiar to these islands. The agronomist Bernat Canyelles tells me that 'one of the most popular fruits to eat with bread & oil and mild cheese were the cherries known as *cireres de sarró*. The *sarró* was a little straw basket with a lid which shepherds would wear around their necks and in which they'd carry their lunch. This was the only kind of cherry with a flesh firm enough to withstand a four-hour walk without getting squashed. The *cirera de sarró* was one of the earliest varieties to fruit, dark blood red and sweet, and a very good friend to cheese, as friendly as Muscat grapes. In the market, when anybody brought in a crate of these cherries, they were the first to go.'

The custom of eating fruit with bread & oil, although rich in sensory contrasts and healthy properties, was by no means born of a jaded palate: 'I think it was more a case of filling that part of the stomach that always seems to be empty. It wasn't so much for the pleasure of it as to satisfy the hunger.'

The only fruit trees planted in the olive groves were *serveres*, service trees; in autumn their leaves give a splash of gold in the sea of grey-green. (Fig trees, although also a dry-crop, were kept well away because their long-reaching roots would appropriate all the ground moisture.) The cherry-sized *serva* or serb-apple, a relative of the rowan, ripens at the beginning of October. It can be eaten only when it has fallen to the ground and bletted, that is, turned brown and soft to the touch. You can nip a hole in the skin with your teeth and squeeze the sweet, nutty custard out like toothpaste. The olive-pickers would eat it with their bread & oil.

If you shy away from the idea of mixing sweet and savoury, consider the avocado. It contains more protein than any other fruit, B-complex vitamins and also vitamin A which is only present in certain fatty foods. It's too bad it wasn't acclimatized to these latitudes in our grandparents' day, because it could have supplemented the scarcity of vegetable protein. Protected from the wind and with plenty of water, it produces excellent fruit in this climate. A few slices of avocado are a great complement to a vegetarian *pa amb oli*, but go easy on the oil because twenty-five per cent of the avocado pulp is mono-unsaturated fat, almost as much as the olive itself. The avocado has to be soft to the touch before it's edible, normally a few days after it's picked from the tree, no matter at what stage of the growing season. The name, incidentally has nothing to do with lawyers; the root is the word *ahuacatl* which, I understand, means 'testicle' in the ancient Aztec language.

Dried fruit

One of the distant voices still resounding in the babble of our ancestral diet is the Arab taste for combining sweet with savoury. 'We love this conjunction of tastes: the *cocarrois*,[9] baked fish *à la mallorquina*, pork or thrushes wrapped in cabbage leaves, eaten with pine kernels and raisins; *ensaïmades*[10] with *sobrassada* and *carabassat*[11] …My grandfather used to eat early figs or grapes with his *sopes*. All this you find more in the Levant, you won't find it so much in the mountains. There's an abyss between a *Solleric* and a *Mancorí…*'

In the Arab world, the habit of eating dried fruit is widespread, especially among nomadic tribes dependent upon dates, raisins, prunes, dried apricots, fig-bread, almonds and pine nuts as a concentrated and long-lasting source of proteins and minerals. From Rabat to Teheran, passing through the ex-Arab colony of Mayurqa, you'll find dried fruit forming a part of fish, meat and rice dishes. It also forms a part of *pa amb oli* culture.

'How was it possible,' muses Antoni Pinya, 'for the olive pickers to hold out for a full working day against the freezing December winds, on the high olive groves of the Tramuntana mountains, on a simple diet of bread & oil? The answer is simple: it was eaten with a slice of fig-bread—pressed figs and aniseed—which could provide 500 calories.'

---

[9] 'Kings pie', a semicircular pasty stuffed with spinach or cauliflower and raisins.

[10] A spiral of sweet puff pastry made with lard.

[11] Crystallized pumpkin.

When meat and dairy products were scarce, raisins or dried apricots were also a useful winter supply of sugars and minerals.

Pa amb patata

While investigating *pa amb oli* culture, I've come across a few curious combinations, all the more curious when I discovered they were habits shared by various members of a family, village or social group. One such habit, which defies all alimentary logic yet appears to be fairly widespread among immigrants from Andalucia or Extremadura, is the *pa amb oli* with *tortilla española*. A piece of Spanish potato omelette can be a gob-stopper when eaten on its own; on a slice of bread & oil, it's a riot of carbohydrates. A 'light' version, popular among certain groups of urban teenagers, is the *pa amb oli 007*, named after a local brand of potato crisp. It consists of two slices of bread & oil & scrubbed tomato, sandwiching half the contents of a packet of crisps. It's an explosion of contrasting flavours—cheese & onion, smoky bacon—and textures, often followed by the explosion of a gastric depth-charge.

The miracle of the loaves and fishes

As you wander out of the cinema, you bump into a group of friends you haven't seen in a long time.

'Hey, we're blocking the pavement; let's all go somewhere and get a bite to eat.'

'Why not come to my place, we'll pick up a bottle along the way and make a *pa amb oli*…'

It's that simple. If you are a serious *pambolier*, at home you'll always have a string of tomatoes, a farmhouse loaf, a litre or two of virgin oil and a bag of Inca biscuits on hand, as well as olives or pickles. If there's enough appetite, friendship and wine to go around, that's all you need. But socially, bread & oil can be a lot more than a spontaneous fix-it; it can be the basis of a New Year's Eve party, or a sophisticated buffet-supper with an informal feel to it. You can prepare the bread & oil yourself beforehand (not too soon, lest the bread becomes soggy) or have the slices, oil, salt and tomatoes ready on a tray and let the guests fix up their own, which is a good way for them to break the ice. What's more, a *pa amb oli* party has the advantage of adjusting itself to the circumstances: if the guests are hungrier than you catered for, or if your teenage son brings the gang over, another loaf and a raid on the larder will put things right. If, on the other hand, half the guests don't show up, the left-overs can keep or be recycled over the rest of the week's meals. Bread & oil is also a good basis for a flat-warming or student party: when your budget is too tight to invite everybody to a slap-up meal, just provide the basics and ask your guests to bring, apart from the proverbial bottle, whatever they can: a tin of sardines, a jar of pickles, a piece of cheese, a salami or chorizo, some smoked salmon…

The painter Laetitia Bermejo, who did the line drawings for this book, explains a typical communal bread & oil: 'We were a group of friends, artists and such, who were employed building and painting the sets for a TV docudrama about Lady Diana, being shot entirely on the island. The interiors were built and filmed in the old butane gas depot in the olive groves above Fornalutx. We were working against the clock, and we'd all eat together, painters and carpenters—Toni de Cúber, Zappa, Michael Kane, Jeannot and the rest. It was freezing cold outside, and the caretaker of the olive groves, Leandro *"Pastilla"* would make a fire in a wheel-barrow under the porch, so we could keep warm and dry. We'd toast the bread over the embers, and each lay out the food we'd brought along, an amazing variety, which wasn't surprising considering the mixture of people in that team, Majorcans, mainlanders and foreigners. The most delicious combination I tasted was a slice of bread toasted over the embers on one side; this was scrubbed with tomato and doused with olive oil, spread with *sobrassada* paste and topped with a slice of camembert. Then we'd toast the other side and the *sobrassada* and camembert would begin to melt together. What a bomb!'

Wine

'The drink that best complements a *pa amb oli* is red wine, and the obvious choice would be one of our Majorcan *vins negres*, which are improving in quality every year. Maybe in the summer you'd prefer a cold beer rather than a chilled white wine, unless you're eating fish with your bread & oil, in which case a Blanc Pescador or a Viñasol would do nicely.'

'What to drink with bread & oil? If it's accompanied by cold meat or cheese, red wine; if anchovies or tuna, beer or white wine. Not so long ago, it was almost an offence to ask for mineral water with your *pa amb oli*, but now people order it as much as alcohol,' says the barman at the Moka Verd.

'But wine aids the digestive process, whereas water doesn't, and beer can have the opposite effect.'

A local red Binissalem wine has a hint of astringency that clears the palate and can compensate for an excess of oil, in the way a jasmine tea is taken with a Chinese meal.

At Ca n'Amer, one of the best known *cellers* in Inca, I'm told: 'The cured meats and cheese produced on the islands call for a local red wine, made from Majorcan *manto negro* grapes. The regulating body of the *Denominació d'Origen de Binissalem* insists that their wines contain from seventy per cent to eighty per cent of juice pressed from this variety. A Binissalem wine is more robust than a Rioja or a Ribera del Duero, it has more body and is a little tarter. It's not as mild as a wine made from *cabernet sauvignon* or *tempranillo* grapes, it's a strong brew that complements the strong flavours of the local cheeses and cold meats, it's a nice balance of power. If you were to eat a well-cured Mahon cheese with a wine made from Merlot grapes, the cheese would overpower it, and the wine wouldn't clean your palate.

'Wine is not only a healthy complement to bread & oil, it's even recommended by many cardiologists. Today we know that the black grape and the wine it produces is one of the best anti-carcinogenics in nature, as good or better than other antioxidants like broccoli, celery or parsley. The benefits of a glass of red wine shouldn't be disdained on account of the few degrees of alcohol it contains.'

Choosing wine can be an enjoyable pastime or a very expensive blunder. Majorcan wines have evolved enormously. Ten years ago, most shops would only stock Copinya, José Ferrer's Binissalem Autèntic and Franja Roja, and those four-litre refillable carafes of pugnacious Santa María. (Mother of God, fourteen degrees!) Today the range of good local wines is enormous, we have two *denominacións d'origen*, Binissalem and Pla i Llevant.

Jaume Mesquida of Porreres has even begun to bottle the first local *cava*. Our village mayor confesses, 'before my operation I was always in too much of a hurry to enjoy a quiet *pa amb oli*. My enforced repose opened my eyes to the possibilities of bread & oil with a brut cava, a perfect combination.'

At the back of the book you'll find a Majorcan wine list.

Non-alcoholic beverages

Those who don't, can't, shouldn't or won't drink alcohol, will usually drink mineral water with their *pa amb oli*; few will opt for a Coke or other sweet fizzy drink. Personally, if I can't handle a sip of wine with my elevenses, as is usually the case, a fresh orange or lemon juice fits the bill quite nicely. If I'm in a bar and a fresh juice is going to cost more than the *pa amb oli* itself, I'll order one of those lemon-tea concoctions which is the least sweet of the soft drinks and has a touch of astringency.

Here in Spain we are well behind northern Europe as far as adult non-alcoholic drinks are concerned. There's plenty of alcohol-free beer, Red Bull for the ravers and isotonic concoctions for the workers-out, but the more sophisticated drinks of the elderflower-and-ginseng variety, an interesting option for bread & oilers, have yet to catch on.

'When times are hard, no bread is stale.'

NEW DIRECTIONS

Chapter 8

Contemporary Trends in the Characteristic Behaviour of the *Homo Balearicus Pamboliensis* in a post-Espadrille Society

Paper submitted by Dr Pamela 'Pam' Bollie of the Breadnoil Institute of Massachusetts before the XXV Congress of the International Mediterranean Diet League.

In order to build up a database of pambolistic habits, with the aim of presenting my findings before my learned colleagues present in this XXV Congress, I prepared a questionnaire which was distributed among two hundred and twenty five adult Majorcans and long-term residents on the island. Those who received a copy were public figures representing the worlds of politics, business, culture, sport and—given the Biblical connotations of the subject at hand—of the Church.

The clearest conclusion I could draw from this survey confirms a hypothesis which I had put forward in an earlier paper. The hypothesis is this: adult Majorcans—and, I suggest Balearic islanders in general—abhor answering questionnaires. Of those who didn't respond to mine (the majority of those who received it), I'd like to elucidate the motives for their lack of cooperation. A small percentage, who in principle were well disposed towards the subject of the survey, declined because it was written in Imperialist Spanish. Another group, upon discovering a stamped addressed envelope enclosed, put it aside at the very thought of going out to find a letterbox. The rest acted in consequence with their practical and insular character, using my questionnaire to light the stove or to jam it, folded in four, under the short leg of the kitchen table. Among politicians, I've received more response from the right wing than the left, who were obviously too busy to waste time with this kind of nonsense. Good for them.

To sum up: only one in six questionnaires were answered and returned. I'm forced to admit that my survey lacks scientific rigour and that any statistician would reject my database; nor would any scientific journal dare to publish my findings. However, the whole exercise took up a lot of time and energy, not to mention the cost of the stamps and photocopies, so I certainly didn't want my study to end up in a bottom drawer. Besides which, I couldn't miss the opportunity of attending this congress, since the Institute was paying for my trip and expenses.

Here, then are my findings:

How frequently do you eat a pa amb oli?
66% – One or more times a week.
21% – Daily.
10% – No regular frequency.
 3% – Not specified.

At what time of day do you usually fancy eating a pa amb oli?
43% – At suppertime.
 6% – Breakfast.
 6% – Mid-morning.
 6% – At all hours.
34% – Depends upon the day.

Nobody admitted to lunching on *pa amb oli*, but five per cent considered the possibility of eating one at mid-afternoon, a figure which would have increased considerably had we reduced the lower age limit of the sample to include school children.

Where do you normally eat pa amb oli?
67% – Only at home.
13% – Only at an establishment specializing in *pa amb oli*.
10% – At home or in a bar (one subject specified the Moka Verd).
 6% – Wherever I happen to be.
 3% – Not specified.

Which kind of bread do you prefer?
54% – Brown Majorcan bread (*pa pagès*).
26% – White Majorcan bread (*pa mallorquí*).
 3% – Whole-wheat bread.
 3% – *Llonguet.*

One of the subjects, Gabriel Cañellas Fons, ex-president of the Balearic Government, was very specific: in seventy per cent of cases, he would choose brown bread and in the remaining thirty per cent, a *llonguet.*

The French loaf or bread roll, although the basis of most *pa amb olis* served in normal bars, was even less popular than whole-wheat. As for other options, twelve per cent mentioned *chapata* or *ciabatta* bread as a second choice and six per cent a whole-grain loaf. One subject specified the following: 'a hand-made *panet d'oli* without the usual glacé sugar dusting, toasted or not, pierced along both channels and the oil poured into both the holes; or, in pieces, sponging up the oil from a puddle in the bottom of a soup-plate.'

In which order do you apply the basic elements (scrubbed tomato, oil, garlic, salt) to the bread?
One third of the subjects use garlic; of these, eighty per cent apply it first and the remaining twenty per cent last. The rest of the elements are applied as follows, in order of popularity:

1. Tomato, salt, oil.
2. Tomato, oil, salt.
3. Oil, tomato, salt.
4. Salt, oil, tomato.
5. Salt, tomato, oil.
6. Oil, salt, tomato.

The subjects were presented with four hypothetical models of *pa amb oli*: bread toasted or not, tomato scrubbed or laid on in slices. Some altered it depending upon the case, others always maintained the same order. A few found my options limiting: two subjects specified 'oil first and again last', one 'tomato first and last'.

When preparing a pa amb oli, *how do you consider yourself?*
78% – Traditionalist, purist.
 3% – Innovative, experimental.

7% – Neither one nor the other.
9% – Couldn't say.
3% – Hedonist.

Which savoury foods usually accompany your pa amb oli?
40% – Cheese.
23% – Ham (cured or cooked).
20% – Anchovies, tuna, etc.
 3% – Other cured meats.
18% – I prefer my *pa amb oli* straight.

This question also offered the option 'other...' which elicited the following suggestions (in order of popularity): *esclatasangs* (a wild mushroom, *Lactarius deliciosus*), boiled beef, lamb chops, omelette, chopped hard-boiled egg, dried tomato, *escalivada* (strips of roast red pepper and aubergine in oil and garlic).

Indicate your favourite savoury garnishes in order of preference:
50% – Majorcan olives (*verda, trencada, pansida, blava*).
28% –Vinegar pickles (samphire, capers, gherkins, etc).
11% – Olives from the mainland (Seville olives, plain or
          anchovy-stuffed, etc).
10% – Raw vegetables.

In the 'other...' section, entries included fresh herbs (marjoram, rocket, watercress, wild garlic), ginger, *gomasio* (sesame seeds ground with salt) and Japanese miso or iziki seaweed.

Have you eaten pa amb oli *with something sweet?*
46% – with grapes.
23% – with fresh figs.

13% – with sugar.

6% – (each register) pomegranate, orange,
     codonyat (quince jelly).

'Others…' include peeled prickly pear, apple, pear, *sobrassada* fried with honey, and *turrón* (a Christmas sweet akin to nougat and marzipan).

Do you consider that bread & oil, with its traditional accompaniments, can form the basis of a balanced and healthy diet?
63% – Yes.
3% – No.
34% – Don't know.

Among those who answered 'yes', several subjects went further: 'yes, despite the risk of getting fat'; 'as a basis, yes, but you'd have to add fruit, vegetables and legumes'; 'the base, yes, and the peak as well'; 'in fact I know many older people who eat it for supper every day of the year'; 'yes, and I think it's even possible to get hooked on it'.

What do you normally drink with your pa amb oli?
35% – Wine.
33% – Wine, water.
20% – Beer.
3% – Fresh lemon or orange juice (seasonal).
3% – Cold milk.
3% – Nothing at all.

What, in your opinion, is the difference between the Balearic pa amb oli *and the Catalan* pantumaca *or* pa amb tomàquet? *(The big one!)*
12% – Don't know.

10% – Essentially, there is no difference.

27% – The difference is in the bread: 'In Catalonia, the bread is spongier, and when you try and rub the tomato on, you wreck it'; 'the *pa amb tomàquet* leans more heavily on the accompaniment—ham, *botifarra*, or whatever—while the secret of the Balearic *pa amb oli* is the bread itself, which is unsurpassable'; 'here the bread is really good and there it's like chewing gum'; 'Catalan bread is splendid with tomato and oil'.

14% – The tomato: 'the *pantumaca* has the tomato on both sides of the slice', 'over there they reduce the tomato to a pulp and apply it with a paint-brush'.

6% – The oil: 'They've got absolutely nothing in common, the Majorcan oil gives ours a very special taste'; 'you just have to compare the names: here, the most important element is the oil, over there it's the tomato'.

5% – This group shows its true colours, affirming that 'the Balearic *pa amb oli* is much better' (this from our ex-president); 'anything Majorcan has to be better', 'the ingredients of a *pa amb tomàquet* don't have the quality of Balearic products'.

Other comments include those who consider that the difference resides in 'the *porró*' (the Catalan wine carafe), in 'the presentation' or 'the anchovies from l'Escala.' One of the subjects declares that the difference between the *pa amb oli* and the *pa amb tomàquet* 'is the same as the difference between the Valencian paella and the Stockholm paella.'

(This might be the moment to include a professional point of view. Xisco Cortés, manager of Amano Bar, points out that 'a complete *pa amb oli* like we serve here, with brown bread and scrubbed *tomatiga de ramellet*, has nothing in common with the Catalan *pa amb tomàquet* which is made with white bread, garlic and salad tomato or even tomato purée and is served in restaurants as a starter. Our *pa amb oli* is a complete breakfast or supper, not an appetizer to eat with your lunch. They are different concepts.')

Do you think that with good marketing, the authentic pa amb oli *could be accepted and adopted outside the Balearics?*
57% – Without a doubt.
33% – Possibly.
10% – With difficulty.

Among the commentaries, we find the following: 'Yes, but… is it in our interest for that to happen?'; 'more than marketing the *pa amb oli*, we should think about exporting the ingredients'; 'it will all depend upon the translation of your book'; 'let's hope that the authentic *pa amb oli*— without sticking this label on it—stays here on the islands.'

Where, or under what circumstances, did you eat your most memorable pa amb oli*?*
The *pa amb oli de tafona* has impressed quite a few. Gabriel Cañellas, politician: 'In the old days, when oil presses were common in all the *possessions*, they would soak toasted bread in the vat of virgin oil. Once I had occasion to taste it and I've never been able to forget it.'

Damià Caubet, journalist: 'Mine was in the oil press at Can Puigserver; some slices of toasted bread, soaked in virgin oil of about 5°, with fried baby thrushes.'

Antonia Serrano, writer from Valldemossa: 'I think back on the bread toasted on the furnace of the oil press at Ses Cases Noves, on the Deià road, and then dipped into the vat of virgin oil. A pinch of salt on top and my fingers impregnated with the aroma of the best oil in the whole Serra de Tramuntana.'

'There are very few places where they can make you a *pa amb oli* the way it should be made, even though it's simple enough', says the composer of contemporary music and director of the ACA Foundation, Toni Caimari. 'Other than at home, the most memorable was at the Can Gras cafè in Binissalem.'

Pere Joan, a friend and illustrator, remembers all the *pa amb olis* he has eaten at Cas Batle Negre (The Black Mayor's) in Banyalbufar. 'Not that there's ever been a black at the head of the Banyalbufar Town Council, but there was a fair-headed mayor who would alternate with another chap, and to distinguish them, the other was nicknamed *Es Batle Negre*, and the bar is named after him. Recently, at some friends' house, I had a memorable *pa amb oli* as a New Year's Eve supper, with all the trimmings.'

Xavier Pastor, a Majorcan who is president of Greenpeace in Spain: 'One winter, in the middle of a motorcycle trip with a group of good friends, in Orient. I've also eaten memorably at the Taberna de la Boquería, near Sa Llotja in Palma.'

Other remarkable *pa amb olis* eaten away from home: 'at Ca Na Punta in Sa Ràpita: bread & oil, figs and roast *botifarró*'; 'a cheese *llagosta* at the Bar Bosch in Palma'; 'a mixed *pa amb oli* at the Cafetí…'

The one that is etched on the memory of the writer Vida Gabriela was in Son Beltran in Deià, 'while listening to the *gallufes* sing as they rested for breakfast beneath the fig tree close to Es Pins.'

For Victor Uris, blues musician, 'a good *pa amb oli* can turn any good day into a memorable day.' Toni Nicolau, of the rock group Occults, eats 'the most memorable one of my life every day', while for his brother Jaume it was 'at home, with *esclatasangs* grilled over the embers.'

Jaume Anglada, our answer to Springsteen, always enjoys eating bread & oil in any village on the island, but 'the one that comes to mind was quite weird: finding myself in Madrid and trying to explain to the waiter that I wanted oil and tomato on my bread. I asked myself: don't they even know what a *llonguet* is in this town? How can they make something as simple as a *pa amb oli* be so complicated?'

Another person impressed by bread & oil overseas is Guillem Timoner, world-champion cyclist, who remembers eating one 'in Taiwan, at the home of my in-laws, who, sadly, are now deceased.'

My sister Lucia, author and translator, explains on the other hand, that 'every time I return to the island after a while abroad, the first thing I do is make myself a *pa amb oli*. Until that moment, I can't be sure I'm really back.'

Sometimes it's the company or the occasion that makes it memorable: Bernat Reüll, of our most internationally-travelled group, Els Valldemossa, remembers 'sharing a *pa amb oli* with Robert Graves at his house.' For the poet Toni Rigo, 'the best *pa amb oli* is the one you eat beside the one you love', while the American writer Foster Grunfeld, brought up here, declares 'the most memorable one was in 1969, the time I seduced a Swedish girl with the help of a *pa amb oli*.'

For many of those questioned, the best is always home-made; for Tolo '*Güell*' Barceló, organizer of the annual nocturnal march to Lluc, 'at my bar, Can Güell, in the company of friends.' For Dr Carles Amengual, president of the Spanish Homeopathic Association, 'I eat the most memorable one of my life every evening at home; the hungrier you are, the better it is.' The politician Damià Pons has tasted 'the best at home, made by yours truly.' For Jaume Matas, President of the Balearic Islands at the time this questionnaire was sent out, the most memorable was 'at home with my family.' Gaspar Sabater, journalist, painter and press secretary at the Balearic Parliament, agrees and adds that 'restaurants in general don't know how to make it properly.'

A memorable meal of bread & oil is a cumulus of experiences and feelings, sensory as well as sentimental; it may rekindle childhood memories or remind one of an encounter the day before yesterday; it can be a solitary pleasure or a social occasion.

Thank you for your attention. Any questions?

Chapter 9

Bread and oil
&
rock and roll

We're burning the midnight oil
We're breaking the holy bread
We're gonna salt your wounds
With some rock 'n roll tunes
Rockin' till we raise the dead.
(Pa Amb Oli Band) .

At the end of the sixties, the cafés in our village closed at eleven at night, so the party would move on to someone or other's house. The music was funky or Latin, played on a Philips portable gramophone, and when the batteries gave out the music would continue with a guitar and whatever percussion could be found in the kitchen. These jam sessions were loosely translated as *sesions de pa amb oli*. At a village fiesta in 1971, some of us offered to put the music to the Miss Local Tourism contest, and formed a one-night group calling ourselves Pa Amb Oli.

In 1978 the English painter David Templeton settled

down in the village. He earned a living doing twenty-minute portraits of the tourists in the hotels at Magalluf, but his gift for reproducing the essence of a face on paper was complemented by his ability to imitate any voice or accent. He had never sung before in public, but at a party he began to imitate Dylan, Elvis, Lennon and Jagger, while my brother Juan accompanied him on the guitar. In 1979 they performed with a couple of French musicians at the Pension Mundial Can Quet. The band was billed again as Pa Amb Oli, a name which had by now become a catch-all for any local musical activity.

On April 11th 1980, *¿Por Qué No? Productions* (promoters of local artists Kevin Ayers, Offbeats and Sex Beatles) organized a gig at the St Germain club in Port de Sóller; the flyer announced, for the first time, The Pa Amb Oli Band. The name and original line-up still rocks today: Tomás and Juan Graves, bass and guitar, Dave Templeton, vocals and Jordi 'Ramone' on drums. The song-list was mainly rock 'n roll standards. Twenty years have gone by and the song list is still mainly rock 'n roll but we've performed over a thousand different ones. We've had such illustrious guests and regulars as Joan Bibiloni, Ramón Farrán or Ollie Halsall on drums, Kevin Ayers and Archie Leggett on bass, Michael Sheffrin and Mike Oldfield on guitars, Hugo Napier, Jeremy Lynton and Paul Matthews on sax, while on vocals guests include Frances Baxter, Tamsin 'Babar' and Samuel 'Blob' Gough, Mike McDonald, Charlie Ainley, 'Little' Charles Walker, Eric Burdon, Hamish McDonald, Rachel Ayers, Curtis Jones, Natalia Farrán, Sarah Jane Morris or Catherine Zeta-Jones; on percussion Phil Shepherd and Carmen GGG, and Dito Vidal on harmonica.

Over the years we've played the better part of a

thousand rock classics in hundreds of gigs: sleazy empty
music bars or packed sweaty pubs, all-night village fiestas
(in which it's normal to go on-stage at 5 a.m.), benefit
concerts, weddings and birthdays, even a couple of gigs for
a captive audience at Palma jail. And us musicians, often
drunk and sleepy but inspired and connecting with the
people; out of tune or out of key, forgetting how to end a
song or surprising ourselves by playing a request perfectly
without ever having rehearsed it; ending a concert with a
good part of the audience on stage singing the chorus to
Twist And Shout (once, with a couple of Guardia Civil to
boot, trying to keep order). And as we pack up, the dawn
breaking over the broken glass and empty bottles, the die-
hards asking for one more song, drunkenly singing,

> *Volem pa amb oli*
> *pa amb oli volem*
> *i si no ens en donen, no mos anirem!*[1]

To date, we've never gone into the studio to record; for us,
canned classic rock 'n roll is like sliced bread. Once we
went to play for the *quints*[2] in a village in the tomato-
growing part of the island, and after setting up we went to
the nearest cafè for a light supper of bread & oil.

At the table behind us, four old codgers were playing
dominoes, and had seen our posters: 'I've heard that these
people don't sing in Majorcan, they don't even know how
to play a *bolero mallorquí*, and yet they think they can come
here and lecture us about *pa amb oli*.'

Well, gents, that's exactly what I've come to do. I'm the

---

[1] 'We want *pa amb oli* and we won't leave until we get it!' (See preface.)

[2] Every year, the town's youths who are eligible for military service organize
a farewell party before leaving for the barracks.

only member of the band who doesn't have an olive grove to care for (my orchard is full of fruit trees) but over the years I've picked enough olives at home to know what it's all about.

This book started life as a project between the five members of the Pa Amb Oli Band; since we had no record, we thought it would be fun to put together a scrapbook for the punters, with posters, song-lists, anecdotes and some favourite bread & oil recipes to fill the pages. But the project was too much like hard work and the band, who find it difficult just organizing a rehearsal, let it ride. I revived the idea of a *pa amb oli* book when my publisher asked for a follow-up to *A Home in Majorca*, but it turned out the opposite of the original project; only three per cent about the musicians, and the rest about food. Anyway, let me introduce the band:

Jordi 'Ramone' Rullan, drums. He's the captain of the fishing boat Dolores based in Sóller port. His father left off fishing for a few years to run the Bar Las Palmeras in Deià, and bought Jordi his first drum kit at the age of sixteen. Jordi began to play with the new-wave Offbeats; they went to London to seek their fortune but the adventure came to an inglorious end with Jordi's kit being retained as back-rent for a rehearsal room in Camden Town. Jordi went back to the family business of fishing, but his heart has never stopped beating out that BLAP'M-BLAP'M-DISHHH. He rejoined the Pa Amb Oli Band in 1986.

'To make a *pa amb oli* mariner, a seaman's bread & oil, we take a bowl and roughly slice green pepper and white onion into it, with salt and oil, as if for a *trempó* salad, and slices of bread rubbed with *tomàtiga de ramellet*, or with sliced tomato if there's no hanging tomatoes available. On another plate we lay out some fried fish, *gerret*[3] or *molls*,[4] and eat the two together, quicker than fast. If there's a lot of work on the boat, like when we're fishing *llampuga*,[5] there's no time to sit down and eat it, so most of it ends up going overboard to feed tomorrow's catch.'

David 'Bon Temps' Templeton, lead vocals and harmonica. He has exhibited his oils and collages all over Europe. 'At Ca's Bernats I look after the farm animals; we make our own oil, cultivate a vegetable garden and an avocado orchard, so I got into the habit of eating *pa amb oli* and avocado for breakfast every day. We don't string up our *tomàtigues de ramellet*, we hang the sprigs on pomegranate branches whose thorns are perfect for this purpose.'

Dave suggests laying a thin slice of Emmental on your bread & oil and putting it under the grill for a couple of minutes. He also recommends eating it with scrambled eggs.

Juan 'Johnny Caprini' Graves, rhythm guitar. Photographer, tree-pruner and founder of the group, Juan cultivates two olive groves and several carob trees. He is also the local representative of the Balearic Federation of Slingers, and regional sub-champion of this sport. He's a purist, both in rock 'n roll and bread 'n oil: 'I never go easy on the oil. I don't have time for this business of pouring the trickle of oil over the slice, because it doesn't spread out evenly. I pour it directly onto the plate and lay the slice of toasted bread face down on top of it, so that it soaks it

---

[3] The picarel, a kind of sardine (*Spicara smaris*).

[4] Red mullet (*Mullus surmuletus*).

[5] Dolphin fish (*Coryphaene hippurus*).

up like a sponge, turn it over again, and then it's ready for the tomato. When fennel is in season—which is from October to June—I chop up some shoots from the plant outside my kitchen door and sprinkle it over the bread & oil.'

Tomás 'Tommy Tombs' Graves, bass guitar and backing vocals, is a typographic designer, hand-printer and the author of this book. 'My wife Carmen (who occasionally plays tambourine with the band) and I always eat toasted whole-wheat bread & oil around half past eleven. It's a good opportunity to get rid of leftovers from the fridge or larder, but there's always a good Majorcan or *maonès* cheese on hand, some herb salt, home-made chutney, pickled onions or beetroot, some *crudités* and a thimbleful of red wine.'

Dai Griffiths, who joined the band in 1996 on lead guitar and backing vocals, is a computer consultant. He married the daughter of a Deià farmer when she was visiting his native Wales in the early 1970s. Now living here, they look after the family olive groves and have planted a vineyard of *malvasia* grapes to make Malmsey wine. The farm's oil press ceased operations when the mule died of shock after a tremendous fireworks display at the Hotel La Residencia which resounded throughout the valley almost causing a rock-slide.

'When the first British mountaineers climbed the Himalayas, one of the most terrible privations they were forced to suffer was caused by the fact that water boils at a lower temperature the higher you climb. Britain, of course, is a very low-lying country and in consequence God saw to it that tea would attain its maximum quality when infused in water at 100° centigrade. Water cannot be heated beyond boiling point, which at the top of the Himalayas isn't high enough to extract the full flavour of those poor mountaineers' favourite brew.

'Here in Majorca, we find the opposite to be true, since the divine scheme has disposed that, given the Majorcan taste for excursions, the flavour of bread & oil increases with every metre one climbs the *serra*. Consequently, the best *pa amb oli* that a native of Deià can taste must of course be eaten on the summit of the mountain which overlooks the village, the *Teix*. One has to make a little campfire out of twigs collected on the way up through the evergreen oak forest, toast a good slice of bread and douse it in local olive oil. My preference is for a thin slice of *jamón serrano* grilled for a few seconds over the embers, which compensates for the fact that I forgot to bring the salt. At this altitude, the tomato—so indispensable at sea level—is entirely optional.'

Chapter 10

On the road with bread & oil

I'm sick to death of *xiringuitos*
They only serve burgers and hot dogs
They only give you chips and shish kebabs
They nearly nearly nearly make you forget

That what you want is bread & oil
a *pa amb oli* with Sóller olives
That what you want is bread & oil
a *pa amb oli* with *maonès* cheese
a *pa amb oli nacional*

Everybody sets up their *xiringuito*
If Majorca turns ugly, you don't give a damn
If Majorca is sick you don't give a toss
Make your dough and brag about it,
    that's what it's all about

Here everyone sets up their *xiringuito*
Hello, how are you? *Togueder* forever,
Wechauchu foki foki[1] *xiringuito*
They nearly nearly nearly make you forget.

---

[1] Phonetic rendition of beach Spanglish.

(From *Pa amb oli nacional*, a local hit by Occults, a rock band from Manacor. Words and music by Antoni Nicolau, reproduced by kind permission. 'I wrote the song in 1990, following the Balearic nationalist penchant for discovering our own identity. We have always been exploited, and here the band is criticizing the ubiquitous sleazy *xiringuitos*— fast food joints, clap-board beach bars, hot-dog stands— and vindicating our own *pa amb oli* [which is NOT the same thing as *pa amb tomàquet*, Catalan centralists please take note!]')

Bread & oil take-away

In the minds of most islanders, bread & oil is intimately linked to the idea of home; everyone agrees that 'there's no *pa amb oli* like Mum used to make.' It was eaten at home because a slice of Majorcan bread bathed in olive oil can't be carried in your pocket. Before tin foil and plastic bags were invented, there was no oil-resistant packaging material easily available. Even so, bread and oil with sugar was the elevenses for thousands of schoolchildren. The oil dripped and stained everything, clothes and exercise books, leaving the pages transparent and the child paying penance for his carelessness—the usual punishment was to kneel face to the wall, arms outstretched like the cross, under the attentive gaze of the Good Jesus and the Generalíssimo.

The journeymen and farmers who took sandwiches to work opted for bread and *sobrassada* because a *pa amb oli* was too messy to carry ready made, and too complicated to make on the job, involving extra paraphernalia: oil bottle, bread knife, plate, tomatoes, napkin, salt-cellar, etc.

In Andalucia and Extremadura they have solved the problem of the portable bread & oil in a different way.

They use a soft roll or small loaf, cut or bite off one end and pull out the crumb with their fingers, leaving the bread hollow; this is then filled with oil, and after a few seconds, what has not been absorbed is poured back into the bottle. The hollow is then stuffed with chopped tomato and the crumb packed back in to act as a stopper, leaving the outside dry and portable. I've seen this done in Jaen on a grand scale, with a half-kilo loaf and a cupful of oil, to be shared among the olive pickers.

Urban bread & oil

The *pa amb oli* has made its way into Balearic urban culture by the hand of the *jamón serrano*. This was thanks to Casa Gonzalo in Gènova (a village just outside Palma), whose maître combined the local bread & oil with the cured ham from his native Andalucia, repeating the success story of the Catalan *pantumacca amb pernil*. A decade before the Majorcan tourist boom, Andalucian workers had flocked to Barcelona to work in industry and had brought their *jamón* with them, which in Catalan is *cuixot* or *pernil*. So why do we Majorcans use the Spanish word '*jamón*' when we could use either official Catalan term? Obviously because, unlike the Catalans, few of us had ever seen the stuff: our warm and humid climate was unsuitable for curing whole legs of ham. Until the Andalucians introduced it in the '60s we never needed a word for it. As Antonia Serrano points out, 'nobody ate ham with their bread & oil in those days. That would have been an unthinkable luxury.' For the immense majority of Majorcans in the 1960s, *jamón* was just another of those imported words with no local equivalent, like *sandwich*, *bratwurst*, *discothèque* or *souvenir*. Today, the bi-lingual nomenclature '*pa amb oli con jamón*' can be found in any of those corner bars in the rough neighbourhoods around Palma, from Son Cladera to Son Roca, and represents the fusion between the Majorcan and mainland popular culture.

Near the *Porto Pi Centre* shopping mall, opposite McDonalds, there's a typical German bar (Dortmund Bier sign outside, etc) with a little blackboard that announces: '*¡¡Auténtico!! Pa amb oli con Jamón.*' Intrigued at the juxtaposition, I went inside to ask what was so *¡¡autentico!!* About it. The owner turned out to be a very amiable Chilean, who showed me his brown Majorcan loaf, his virgin oil from Sóller, his *tomàtigues de ramellet.* I was convinced.

The words *pa amb oli* on a sign or blackboard are a powerful come-on, with a 'product recognition' factor that would be the envy of many an established brand-name. A trade mark supposedly guarantees quality; a *pa amb oli*, on the other hand, can vary tremendously from one establishment to the next.

'There are bars where they make it with slices of hothouse tomatoes which are cheaper than the proper ones. Then they use sunflower oil; the difference in price is so small that I don't know how anyone can be that stingy. I can't believe there are still people who don't know that to make a good *pa amb oli* you should use virgin olive oil, and if it's Majorcan, so much the better. In the past, perhaps the difference in price was greater; today there's no excuse.'

This is the bottom end of the bread & oil spectrum; at the other we find top-of-the-line *pa amb oli* restaurants offering bread & oil alongside Chicken Stuffed with Cheese or Marinated Salmon with Caviar and Sliced Egg. These sophisticated places tend to take good care of selecting authentic basic ingredients, although some are in danger of reaching the point of snobbishness: 'What's sad about most avant-garde culinary movements is they often go over the top. The fashion in luxury restaurants is olive-oil snobbery; you even find oil lists, graded according to their acidity. That's entering a realm which I find a bit ridiculous; only a professional oil taster could possibly distinguish between a 0.4° and 0.6° olive oil.'

Ordering a *pa amb oli* when out on the town can be a lottery. I once lost half a molar in a dry bread roll lightly lubricated with sunflower oil, at a popular sandwich bar in the centre of Palma, which was fortunately around the corner from my dentist. Yet you can strike it lucky in the most unexpected places. In the desolate landscape past Cap Blanc, for example, there's a *xiringuito* on the side of the road which sells tickets to the prehistoric settlement at Capocorb. Nearly all the visitors are tourists, but here you can eat a really good, unpretentious *pa amb oli* in generous helpings.

For as far as anybody can remember, any corner café in or outside Palma would fix you up with a *pa amb oli* without having to advertise the fact. But since we've been swamped by a flood of impersonal and alienating cafeterias which formed the backwash of the tourist wave, the Majorcan customer finds comfort in seeing the words *Pa Amb Oli* because it indicates a place where he'll feel welcome and at ease, and where they'll speak to him in his own language.

I've mentioned Casa Gonzalo, in Gènova, the pioneer of the *pa amb oli con jamón* nearly fifty years ago. One of the original cooks there was Jacinto, who then opened his own Casa Jacinto close by; this was followed by Can Pedro, and Gènova became the place for Palmesans to drive up to for a meal. Some villages, like Esporles and Palmanyola have become dormitory towns; Gènova has turned into a refectory town. It is to Palma what Segovia is to Madrid: a short drive from the capital, but distant enough to maintain its identity. Most of these restaurants have taken Gonzalo's lead in serving *pa amb oli con jamón* as an entrée, in the Catalan style. It wasn't until the 1980s that music bars and cafés frequented by the young began to serve it as a full but reasonably-priced meal: Sa Ximbomba, also in Gènova, s'Hostal in Montuïri and various cafés around the Santa Catalina market above Palma harbour.

Pa amb oli la nuit

Much of today's urban youth has grown up outside the domestic bread & oil tradition and has only now discovered, through the ever increasing network of *pa amb oli* cafés, a new way of eating healthily while out on the town, without burning a hole in their pocket or liver. Perhaps fifty years from now, today's Palma teenagers will remember end-of-millennium Palma this way:

'Do you remember, darling, that delicious *pa amb oli* we ate in that live music bar near Sa Llotja? *Els Pardals de s'Ase* were playing, before they signed to Virgin, ecstasy was cheaper than wine, and we all ended up in Son Dureta... do you remember Son Dureta, love? That hospital which used to stand where we pick up the space shuttle...? Those were the days!'

Most fast-food restaurants are conceptually based upon a battery-hen farm. Everything is thought out—decor, lighting, music, production lines, fodder that can be swallowed without chewing—to stuff the maximum amount of gizzards as fast, cheaply, hygienically and artificially as possible. The atmosphere is attractive when seen from the street (to capture the customer) but once inside, it is sterile and alienating (so that the customer has no desire to stay once he has finished his food, leaving the seat vacant for the next sucker).

A *pa amb oli* café tends to be conceptually the opposite (following the metaphor, it would be closer to a chicken coop): relaxed, civilized and cosily welcoming, although not much to look at from the outside. It is decorated on a low budget with natural (or at least unpretentious) materials, and discreet lighting; your order is served with proper cutlery, crockery and glassware, and nothing comes in plastic containers. The food is unprocessed and full of vitality inciting the customer to get to grips with it: not just finger-lickin' good, but palm-wiping delicious.

The youth of any nation, to become true citizens of the world, have to transcend their own culture; but to get to that point they first have to assimilate their own, not only intellectually but with all five senses: their music and language, smells, colours, tastes and textures. Bread & oil gives any young Majorcan a solid sense of his roots: island-dwelling, maritime, Mediterranean roots.

I spoke to Iñigo Morales of PIMEM (Majorcan Association of Small & Medium Business) about this recent proliferation of *pa amb oli* cafés on the island. 'It's a youth phenomenon, catering for ages up to about twenty-five. I don't think this clientele is the kind which would make themselves a *pa amb oli* at home; it's a way of spending a Friday or Saturday night on a shoestring. For only 800 pesetas you can eat a generous bread & oil with ham and a glass of wine. More than a fashion, it's a resource. It's also healthy, especially if the bread is toasted, which is less fattening.'

Tomeu Torrens has a different view: 'Someone over the age of thirty-five isn't likely to order bread & oil when they go out for a meal. Normally it's, 'What shall we make for supper? There's nothing in the house… then lets make a *pa amb oli*.' There's no mess in the kitchen, no pots and pans. But when young people come out of work at eight in the evening they don't want to go straight home, they look for a nice reasonably-priced place where they can eat well on a thousand-peseta note and meet up with friends. Many who come over to bread & oil are simply tired of fast food, while others are actually making a political and cultural statement, 'I'm a Majorcan and I don't eat hot dogs!'

'There's a lot of people who still think that the more oil you eat, the fatter you get; you know, "Go easy on the oil, will you!" But if you lead a normal life, if you move about a bit and get some exercise, you won't put on weight. A chocolate bar is more fattening than a quarter of a litre of olive oil! It's like those people who come into your restaurant, order an entrée, main course and dessert, and then demand saccharine for their coffee.

'I think that most people who order bread & oil tend to have a university education or at least have a fairly high cultural standard. That doesn't mean they're in the high income bracket, but they're aware that on a low budget, it's the healthiest way to eat out. You need a bomb-proof stomach to deal with the average pizza dough or synthetic hamburger bun which drops into it like a brick, and then makes you thirsty as hell. A teenage stomach can deal with anything but the day comes when that kind of diet cashes in its chips. At the age of twenty-something, most people begin to look after themselves. The thing about fast food is that it makes everything so easy, with come-ons like McAuto and TelePizza, it's as if they've hooked you by the gullet. Fast food is more adulterated every day and there's no way of knowing what's really in it.

'Hamburgers and chicken nuggets, even though they look solid enough, may contain up to sixty per cent fat disguised as something else. With pizza parlours, it's the same story: real cheese, if it's made properly, is too expensive and would reduce their profit margin. What they usually use is a mixture of powdered milk and other semi-synthetic ingredients. Not only that, we have to take into account all the food additives which are allowed.'

Among the preservatives, colourings, antioxidants, stabilizing and thickening agents, which you'll come across even in frozen ready-to-fry chips, there are several which are known to cause allergies, nausea, nervousness and hyper-activity in children (not to be confused with 'energy'). They can affect your blood pressure, your thyroid gland and cause skin problems. One has to be especially careful of the colouring agents E102–155, the preservatives E210–233, antioxidants E310–321, and the flavour enhancers E 620 and E621. Not all E additives are harmful; under the sinister name E410, an emulsifier used in Philadelphia cream cheese, we discover the gum extracted from our very familiar carob beans!

Trademark fast-food—McThis, Kentucky Fried That and TeleTheOther—appears to be a bargain. But watch out, even at the cheap price, the real cost of the raw materials is ridiculously small, much less than the packaging, marketing and other hidden expenses which don't come into the price of a *pa amb oli*. (In case you're sceptical, by the way, I can assure you that this book is a personal initiative and has no hidden sponsors.)

The raw materials for a *pa amb oli* are, in proportion, immensely more expensive than those used in a pizza or hamburger (as most ethically-produced things usually are), but the final price is similar to a fast-food meal. Several reasons can explain this: there's no expensive trademark one-upmanship, no high-rent prominent locations, and anyone running a *pa amb oli* café is obviously not aiming to get rich quick or to hit and run. The *pa amb oli* itself, being uncooked, is less open to manipulation in the kitchen (no deep frying, microwaving, etc) while the ingredients, preserved using traditional techniques, contain few if any E additives: they usually are what they appear to be.

'At today's prices, a pizza will cost you more, but the ingredients for a *pa amb oli* have to be seen to be of better quality because they aren't disguised beneath a coat of melted cheese,' says Xisco Cortès, who runs the Amano Bar.

'With bread & oil you can't fool the eyes or the palate: everything is up front, and no condiments are used so you can't mask the flavour or lack of it.

'If the cost of the materials varies, it's due to the market price of the hanging tomatoes which can rise six-fold from September to June. If you buy your year's supply of stringed tomatoes in September, you can save a lot of money. With this dish, which anyone can make at home, you can't cut corners by buying cheap ingredients; you have to serve a ham or cheese of a higher quality than the customer would usually buy at the supermarket, so that he really enjoys his meal.

'A *pa amb oli* should be made with slices of brown Majorcan bread, one of those big two-kilo loaves, better if they're toasted; the tomatoes should be *de ramellet*, whatever the price, and olive oil. If you eat it straight, you can use a Majorcan virgin oil, but if it's served with high quality cheese or cold meats, it's best to use a less acid oil so it doesn't smother the taste of a good slice of ham or *camaiot*. Apart from the question of cost, you have to be careful with a strong oil because in this business you get a lot of customers who aren't used to it and some find it keeps coming back on them.'

Most *pa amb oli* joints open only in the evenings, combining the social function of a pub or wine bar, the cultural function of a theatre-café (music, theatre, debates, poetry) and the practical one of a restaurant. S'Hostal in Montuïri began to make spectacular *pa amb olis* thirty years ago, but, one of the owners points out, 'it's only been over the last decade that the partying doesn't stop until well into the wee hours.'

This reflects the island's recent trend in decentralization of night life from the city to the villages, as more young people move back to the rural areas. The bread & oil option allows cafés to offer more than just drinks (and avoid the problem of clients getting drunk on an empty stomach) without having to invest in costly kitchen equipment and space.

'The health authorities don't find much cause for concern when they inspect *pa amb oli* cafés, as long as the kitchen area is clean, because it's a dish which is bought, prepared and served: they don't need to poke about because you can't camouflage anything, it's all up front,' explains Xisco Cortès. 'I've been running the Amano for the last five years, I'm one of the pioneers of *pa amb oli* in the Santa Catalina area. Those who opened the way were Sa Ximbomba in Gènova, and in this neighbourhood it was Es Fonoll, Es Mussol and the Itake Café. If the bread & oil movement goes from strength to strength it's not just on the merits of the food, but because it's served in a very pleasant atmosphere, very much our own. Places like these all have Majorcan character; they offer good company, a good feeling and reasonable prices. I have two regular customers, a five-year-old and an eight-year-old, who prefer to come here than to go out and eat a hamburger.'

In the area around the Santa Catalina market, bread & oil is king, especially on a Friday night when it's almost impossible to find a table in any of the dozens of specialized cafés.

'A few years ago, this neighbourhood was on the decline,' Xisco continues. 'It was a demeaning situation that the people who have always lived here didn't deserve. I really put my weight behind this project; others came along, thank God, and stood beside me. Between us all, what we've achieved is that this area now has a solid future as a centre for bread & oil. This dish is the basis of my business; others have decided to hedge their bets by diversifying their menus.'

Vegetarian bread & oil

'Quite a few vegetarians come to the Amano, because they can share a table with friends who aren't veggies but move in the same milieu.'

When a vegetarian or bread & oilian goes out for the evening he'll look for an intimate place where he can relax, feeding his spirit as well as his body by candlelight, with good conversation, live music, poetry, discussions or theatre. There is now a network of such places, as an alternative to the usual booze-and-head-banging-noise circuit.

'The basis of bread & oil is of course vegan, but a good Majorcan or Mahon cheese comes into most vegetarian diets.'

So, occasionally, does fish, although anything prepared

in wine vinegar is eyed with suspicion. Like intermittent vegetarians, weekend bread & oilians are people who every so often simply need to 'de-tox' from an excess of animal protein and fats that form part of their usual diet.

'We always serve a *pa amb oli* with olives, vinegar pickles and samphire. You can add some radishes or green pepper, but I put some slices of spring onion or garlic. Other places give you a bit of green salad on the side, but for us a *pa amb oli* is a *pa amb oli* and that's that. If it's well made, if you take a little extra care when making it, it can be a full meal. Normally people order wine, but in the heat of summer a plate of bread & oil appreciates the company of a cool beer. But with water? Water and oil don't mix!

'Anyway, if you're still hungry after that, you can order one of our Majorcan desserts, like a *greixonera de brossat* which is a curd cheese in an earthenware pot.'

Autochthonous ingredients

Not long ago, a small place called the Malgrat Café, in a side street opposite the Gran Hotel building, tried a new tack:

'It grew out of a project by some Business Studies students, to set up a shop specializing in the gastronomic produce of the Balearics, especially those made on a family scale, with the possibility of tasting the wares: liqueurs, wines, preserves, cold meats and cheese, even salt. We set it up on a shoe-string, and we chose the *pa amb oli* as the focal point for the venture, being easy to prepare at any time of day. It's also the ideal vehicle for introducing more than a hundred of the registered Balearic farmhouse products to an urban public. Among the Minorcan specialities we have the *carn i xuia*, and of course the *formatge maonès*. In fact we have cheeses from the four major islands, made from goat's, sheep's and cow's milk; all kinds of olives, pickled samphire collected from an islet near Illetes; sun-dried tomatoes preserved in oil with herbs, which is made over near Santanyi... we also have paté made with shrimp, with mushrooms, rabbit, *botifarró*, not to mention spirits such as the Minorcan *gin* (made with juniper berries), the Ibizan *farigola* (a sweet thyme-based liqueur) and the Majorcan *palo* and *herbes*.

'Everybody orders red wine with their bread & oil, even the young girls; I couldn't believe it. Not a single Coke, hardly any beers or rosé wine: everyone orders our *vi negre*.[2] People seem to warm to the fact that we only sell local produce; instead of the usual *pa amb oli amb jamón*, we serve it with *camaiot* or *varia negre*, *butifarró* or *carn i xuia*. People like tasting all these different varieties, so we serve sampler plates. With our cheese sampler we include *jaleo* which is an apple and pumpkin jam which the Minorcans eat with cheese. The combination of sweet and savoury is very much a Balearic habit. We also serve bread & oil with dried fruit: raisins, apricots, almonds, prunes and figs. Our customers aren't only Balearic Nationalists; we get many mainlanders and foreigners. Now we're beginning to get people coming in before work and order a *pa amb oli* with their *café amb llet*, instead of the usual croissant. We always use Sóller oil, it's denser, tastier, sweeter. After so many years of imported oils, most people had lost the taste for it, but they're beginning to recuperate it. The new generation is well disposed towards tasting authentic food; they're well up on the subject, they love everything which is organically grown and locally produced. When they go out, they want quality, not just whatever's quick and easy.

---

[2] The Majorcan red wine can be very dark, which is why we call it 'black wine'.

A *pa amb oli* doesn't take long to make, and you can eat it in a few mouthfuls, but since it's so delicious, it seems to slow you down and get you into a conversation with your friends or with the people at the next table. And since you're feeling relaxed, you have another glass of wine, or a shot of *herbes*, and the conversation comes around to subjects in common, and that's because the bread & oilians tend to be well up on what's happening culturally, in the city or in the villages.'

Educating foreigners

Anyone who thinks that your average *pa amb oli* café only caters to locals and nationalists is way off the mark. 'Here at the Amano we get a lot of outsiders who come in to find out what all this *pa amb oli* business is about; on the half-terms we get lots of groups of students from the mainland, it seems the word is out because they come here straight from the airport. Most Palma people leave town in August, but for us it's the busiest month now that the tourists have cottoned on.'

There are tourists, and tourists. A hotel chef working in Palma Nova explains how he caters for his four hundred Italian clients' craving for bread & oil:

'We put the ripe tomatoes, oil, garlic and salt in the blender, strain out the pips and skin and apply this pulp to the slices of *pa de pagès* with a paint-brush. They love it! When there's any leftover pulp, we add egg and semola of durum wheat to make *pasta al pomodoro*.'

'In parts of Greece', explains Tomeu Torrens, 'which have very similar conditions to ours, an olive oil with 2° of acidity is perfectly normal, but give some to a German to taste and he won't even know if it's olive oil: "Ach, voss iss diss?" You have to work your way in slowly, don't give 'em anything over 1° to start off with. They're beginning to understand that olive oil is healthy and necessary, but they're not ready for the shock of an *oli de tafona* from Sóller. And we must be careful not to let an overly strong oil put them off *pa amb oli* at the outset.'

Any tourist who takes the initiative to explore Palma on his own and discover the local gastronomy is one of the few that actually practices the much-touted 'cultural tourism'. It's quite another thing to convince the package-tourist or lager-lout to try local peasant food.

Na Ruixa, a medium-to-high category restaurant a few metres from the beach of the Port de Pollença, is set to try: 'The peak hours are around supper time; this year we're going to offer *pa amb oli* from nine to five, which is when business is slow. Since we survive basically on our supper clients, we can afford the luxury of trying to introduce a typical peasant *berenar* in an area where eighty per cent of the custom is foreign. Bread & oil will be the basis upon which to introduce other local products. I know what the British and the Germans like, but I don't want to fall into the same old baked-beans-on-toast routine. It's hard to induce the British to try anything new; they'll order sole, knowing it's frozen, rather than try an unknown fresh fish just pulled out of the bay. The Germans don't scare so easily. Their own cuisine is pretty poor next to the French, but it's good home cooking. They love Majorcan food—the *frit*, the *escaldums*, the pork in cabbage leaves—because in Germany they're sick to the back teeth of all that *nouvelle cuisine* stuff. The country's overrun by French and Italian chefs. I think Germans feel more comfortable with our cooking than with anything they find in a restaurant back home. They go crazy when they try our *alioli de patata* which is real Majorcan village food.

'The cured meats that Mateo *Putxer* produces look attractive served alongside a *pa amb oli* and can compete with a board of the most expensive *ibericos*. At Na Ruixa we serve his *camaiot, blanquet* (a white *botifarró*) and the *greixera de porc* (a pork pâté set in an earthenware pot, which is served by the slice).'

In Tomeu's mother's *celler* in Inca, 'we have regular German customers with tremendous spending power—you can tell with a glance at the cars and properties they own—and they come here three times a week to eat good, solid Majorcan home cooking. An Englishman will balk at the sight of a *sobrassada*...'

'An Englishman will balk at the sight of a haggis,' I interject.

'...but a German will plough straight into it. Of course I'm referring more to the foreigners who make a point of enjoying our culture, or have settled down here, not those who come here just to get out of the house for a holiday.'

Malgrat Café has several customers among the foreign residents on the island, who drop in for a bread & oil every time they are in town. 'They wanted to try it and now they love it. It's a good way to get into our Balearic country diet a little at a time; our country cooking can be a bit strong for some foreign palates, and to come face to face with a plate of *frit* might be a traumatic experience for a novice. With *pa amb oli*, he'll first try it with fresh cheese, then with a well cured *maonès*, moving on to a *botifarró*, a *camaiot*, and so on until he'll eventually be ready to face even a pot of snail stew. Foreigners also feel comfortable in a *pa amb oli* café because unlike a *celler* or Majorcan restaurant, there are neither heavily fried foods nor the usual clatter and smell from the kitchen.'

Is the *pa amb oli* an exportable concept? Will we find

branches of the Amano or Sa Llimona in London, Frankfurt and New York? If we have a Japanese restaurant opposite the Santa Catalina market in the heart of *pambolandia*, why not a bread & oilery opposite Tokyo's Central Fish Market? The key is to ensure that the authentic ingredients arrive in perfect condition, which isn't difficult because they keep well. The most delicate ingredient is the *pa mallorquí*, but with the excellent connections between Palma airport and the rest of the world (not to mention overseas, as the Majorcans say), it could be served in London one or two days after baking, when it's at its peak.

The origin of the *llagosta*[3]

Llagosta: a *llonguet* roll cut in half horizontally and toasted, then prepared with olive oil and sliced or rubbed tomato. It is normally served as a hot sandwich, stuffed with cheese, ham, bacon or a combination of these. For ease of eating, it is cut—depending on the establishment—in two along the crease or in three across the crease.

'The name originated one day in 1958, when the *amo*[4] Pep Verd—founder of this café, the Moka Verd—was enjoying the company of some friends at that table over there. After a while he felt the urge to eat a *pa amb oli* but, as luck would have it, behind the bar there was no bread nor *tomàtigues de ramellet*, only a *llonguet* and a salad tomato. As the Orientals say, a setback is always an opportunity in disguise, so *l'amo En Pep* cuts open the *llonguet*, toasts it, gives it the salt and oil treatment, adds a couple of slices of tomato, and closes it. He cuts it into three slices so that his friends can try it.

---

[3] Lobster.

[4] Overseer or man in charge of a farm or estate; used as a term of respectful address, rather like 'Guv'nor' or 'Squire' in English.

'One of them exclaims, "Pep, this tastes better than lobster!"

'One of Pep's cronies was a Palma businessman who would receive a lot of salesmen from the mainland. He would accompany them on their rounds of the shops, and when they got peckish around mid-morning, he'd say, in Castilian Spanish,

'"You know what? Let's go to a bar I know around the corner and order a couple of lobsters."

'"Lobster at this hour of the morning?"

'"Yes, it's the speciality of the house."

'"But… at ten in the morning?"

'"Don't you worry, man."

'And the other chap is already convinced, and says to himself, "Well, well, these islanders… but all right, just for this once, let's make an effort…"

'So they both walk into the Moka Verd and sit down, and the Majorcan says in Spanish to *l'amo En Pep*, "Let's see, Don Pepe, how about preparing us some lobsters?"

'And Pep replies: "Right away!" After a few minutes he returns with the two toasted sandwiches, and sets them down on the table before the incredulous mainlander.

'"But… didn't you order lobster?"

'"Of course! Tuck in!"

'And that's how the *llagosta* got it's name. I know because I was a lad working behind the bar at the time.'

'It's socially acceptable to eat bread & oil with your fingers, even though the Tourism Council obliges us to serve it with knives and forks.'

Chapter 11

Dr Pamboli's Miracle Diet

It was not my intention to write a pseudo-scientific treatise to back up my claims to the excellence of bread & oil, but I thought that including a nutritionist's point of view might lend a certain weight to this book. For a professional opinion, I wrote to my friend Dale Figtree Ph.D., a nutritionist now living in California and author of a book aimed at helping children with obesity problems. She is very familiar with the Mediterranean diet, having lived for years in the Sóller valley, and sent me the following text:

A *pa amb oli* is made from four wholesome, health-benefiting ingredients.

Whole-wheat bread is rich in beneficial fibre, B vitamins and several minerals. Fibre is important for good digestion and is completely removed from 'white' bread.

Olive oil is a fruit oil, pressed from the flesh of the olive fruit rather than its seed. It is a time-tested, health enhancing mono-unsaturated oil. It is more stable and less likely to become rancid than polyunsaturated oils like corn or safflower oil, and because it is unsaturated, it does not contribute to clogged arteries the way saturated fats—such as butter or other animal fats—do. Olive oil is known throughout the Mediterranean to have great health benefits, from maintaining a healthy heart and balanced hormones to good digestion.

Garlic is an age-old folk medicine cure. Pliny said it was a remedy for sixty-one ailments, while Aristotle sang its praises in his writings. It is considered a natural antibiotic which can kill germs and bacteria, and it can rid the body of certain parasites. It is an anti-fungal, it stimulates digestion and can help keep cholesterol at healthy levels.

Tomatoes are rich in minerals and vitamins, especially vitamin C. They are beneficial as blood and liver cleansers, helping to remove toxins and excess uric acid from the body.

Putting it all together, you have *pa amb oli*, not only a delicious but also a nutritious treat.

That seemed to cover it pretty well and I would have ended the nutrition section here, but so much evidence turned up in favour of our bread & oil diet—when healthy and varied ingredients are used—that my notes grew into a separate chapter. I was surprised by the enthusiasm of Pep Tur, a professor of biology at the UIB, who put me in touch with the oncologist Enric Benito, a specialist in the relation between diet and bowel cancer; he in turn introduced me to Dr Marta Puig, who specializes in adolescent nutrition. All three ardently defend the *pa amb oli* culture against the onslaught of fast food.

Even young Majorcan restaurateurs seem to be well up

on the health aspects of the local peasant diet: 'Bread & oil is a really healthy formula, it contains no pernicious fats,' says Tomeu Torrens. 'Clearly, to lose weight we don't have to give up consuming calories like those contained in oil or bread, but we do have to lead a healthy lifestyle with plenty of exercise. Part of the cellulitis problem has its roots in the toxins which accumulate in our bodies after eating processed and adulterated foods, and prevent us from eliminating the water we absorb. The substances which are used industrially to fatten farm animals are passed on to us when we eat their meat. A girl on a diet might refuse a slice of bread & oil in favour of a sliver of boiled ham, which in fact gives her less nourishment and probably more weight. Olive oil and tomatoes are not only healthy, they're necessary. *Pa moreno* gives your body much of the fibre it needs, and is healthier than white bread and, for some people, more appetizing than a heavy whole-wheat loaf. The more refined the flour, the more energy the body has to use to assimilate the carbohydrate chain. The problem today is that the more natural or biologically pure a product is, the harder it seems to be for people to get used to.'

Our best counsellors when it comes to deciding what we should eat or drink, are our hunger and thirst. The body usually recognizes at any given moment what it needs to nourish itself and to maintain its vital functions working properly. 'What I could do with right now…' is a statement of the body's needs in relation to climate, hour of day, age, mental and physical exercise and emotional state. All living creatures are programmed to choose food in this way; in their natural environments, all organisms work well. As an adman would say, 'We're backed by millions of years of experience!' Animals (that includes us) tend to recognize and ingest substances not only for their nutritive value but also for their medicinal, stimulating or tranquillizing effects, upon our metabolism. A cat with intestinal problems will eat grass; a person with emotional problems will get drunk or pig out on chocolate.

A different problem arises when the body is fooled by substances which aren't really what it asked for, whether by omission (foods which have lost their natural properties during processing) or excess (presence of additives, whether natural or chemical). When a kid asks for a hamburger, his body is expecting a certain amount of proteins, carbohydrates, fibre, etc, but what it gets is meat which is two-thirds fat and a bun with less fibre than a microchip. (Lest I give the impression of having suffered some terrible trauma at a hamburger joint, let me make it clear that I could equally point to any other processed and denaturalized food which I occasionally eat. Nor do I deny that there are cases of fraud among supposedly 'organic' products. End of disclaimer.)

At first, the body is easy to fool, especially if the daily doses of the substances it is cheated out of (minerals, vitamins and fibre) or palmed off with (food additives and unnecessary pharmaceuticals) are small. After a time, the cheated party begins to cheat the cheater: the body tells the brain it is satisfied and continues to function apparently normally, until the organic imbalance begins to become evident in another area, namely the weakening of the body's defence mechanism.

Dr Benito describes the impact of diet upon our health from a biological point of view: 'Our structure is genetic, it is conditioned by the inheritance we receive from our parents. That is what makes us susceptible to suffer one illness or another. But all this genetic material we're physically made up of is exposed, during the seventy or eighty years we're alive, to environmental factors. This is a rather mechanist point of view, but it's a part of the truth. These external factors—the air we breathe, the food we eat, what we drink, all our habits—increase the danger of suffering some illness or another.

'The more our diet suits our needs and surroundings, the healthier it is. If we continually eat things which aren't from our own environment, in quantities which bear no relation to the climate we're living in nor our lifestyle and physical needs, it's likely to affect our health because the body isn't genetically prepared to assimilate them. The contradiction of living in a Mediterranean environment and eating a lot of animal fat can affect our health; in some people it manifests itself as a cancer, in others as a coronary or brain disease. The external factors are the same— tobacco, a sedentary lifestyle, eating substances we can't assimilate properly or just plain overeating—but it's our genetic make-up which makes our bodies react in this way or that.'

Every so often new scientific studies are published which force us to revise our way of looking at things. A decade or two ago, olive oil was condemned by researchers as being pernicious to our health; now it's not only vindicated but recommended. *Peix blau* ('blue' fish, including sardines, anchovy, herring) was frowned upon for a time and now it's considered healthy; cow's milk and beef used to be God's gift to mankind and now we have to go easy on them. Etcetera. All this perhaps tells us more about the interests and rigour of researchers, and about the institutions or government agencies who fund them, than it does about the subject of their enquiries. The healthiest diet for any given person—forget about scientific research for a moment—is probably based upon whatever it was his ancestors used to eat: if Norwegian, fish; if Majorcan, vegetables, pulses, olive oil and cereals; if Dutch, dairy products. In the case of the child of a Chinese-Jamaican and an Anglo-Indian, well, he'd better just follow his instinct. But supposing your family is from Sa Pobla and your grandfather used to eat a good plate of *frit* before harnessing up the mule and ploughing two acres, don't expect to live to his ripe old age if you eat the same plate of *frit* every lunch time and spend your working day sitting in front of the computer screen with your backside glued to the chair.

Consumers in general are returning to natural foods, which are no longer a minority option. This is a reaction to genetic manipulation, scandals in the food industry, but also to confusing and contradictory advice coming from marketing boards, health authorities and specialists. Following a healthy diet when you live in a self-supporting commune is fine; reconciling it with today's urban working life requires money, effort and time. Isn't it tempting to buy a microwave-ready meal instead of finding and preparing fresh fish, peeling, chopping and cooking vegetables, seeking out organic products? And if it's difficult to defend a more radical vegan, crudivore or macrobiotic position at home, it's even harder when eating out.

A regular daily dose of real bread & oil is a cheap, quick and easy-to-prepare starting point for giving your body what it really needs, replacing those snacks that give it what it doesn't need: food additives and traces of fertilizers and pesticides. No chemicals are used to make real Majorcan bread and virgin olive oil; there may be traces in the flour, but our olive groves are seldom sprayed, because of the physical difficulty of doing so, and because biological pest control seems to work better in the long run. The hanging tomato needs none of the chemical pampering given to hybrid varieties; the only mineral normally used is copper sulphate powder around the stem of the plant, which, being the basis of Bordeaux mixture, is recognized by various organic agriculture associations.

According to Dr Abel Mariné, one of Spain's leading nutritionists: 'If someone eats hamburger every day, he's not doing himself a favour; the reason is not so much the hamburger itself as the fact that he's following a monotonous diet.' I suppose that the same can be said for a daily *pa amb oli amb jamón*. So let me stress that it's really bread & oil's inherent capacity for firing one's imagination and resourcefulness that makes it a foundation for good health, because a rich and balanced diet depends upon variety.

The Mediterranean diet

The world is being sold the standard northern European or American diet which may well be appropriate for that climate and population, but doesn't necessarily have to suit Haitians, Thais or ourselves. The so-called Mediterranean Diet, however, has been feeding our forefathers for over two millennia, yet it wasn't recognized as a nutritionist concept until 1975, when A. and M. Keys published a study comparing the diets of seven countries (Japan, Finland, Holland, the US, Italy, Greece and Yugoslavia). The authors ventured the opinion that 'the typical diet of the Mediterranean fishermen is the healthiest we know of.'

This diet is based upon cereals, pulses, olive oil, fish, fruit, vegetables and wine. But more than just a repertoire of healthy ingredients, it is a form of (or formula for) life which benefits the body: concepts such as 'let's wait and see what happens' or 'what does it matter', the 'overtable' (as the Spanish so aptly call after-dinner conversation), the siesta and, of course, the regenerative power of the sun. Perhaps the lack of a Protestant work ethic also helps. The Mediterranean diet is not just what we eat, it's what we do, how we do it, and what we are; it all helps to maintain a healthy mind and body.

We should really refer to Mediterranean diets in the plural because among the countries bathed by *Mare Nostrum* there are many differences in customs and habits, as there are within the countries themselves. The winter breakfast of an Aragonese sugar-beet farmer has probably more calories and cholesterol than the daily intake of a fisherman from Andratx; all they have in common is the shot of *anís*. But in spite of these differences, we Mediterraneans in general eat twice as much cereal (bread or pasta with everything) than our northern counterparts. Also more wine, unsaturated oils, fresh fruit and vegetables and pulses. We also eat less meat, animal fat, sweets and dairy produce. If the statistics say the northerners eat as many kilos of vegetables as us, the balance is tipped in their favour by potatoes. Although the area around Sa Pobla is dedicated to exporting potatoes, there are still many Majorcans who don't consider it to be 'real food' but a mere garnish.

How has the Majorcan diet changed over the last eighty years? A study in progress at the UIB has already uncovered some interesting facts. In the early twentieth century, fish and meat together accounted for less than one per cent of the food ingested; today we eat three times as much fish and eleven times as much meat. We eat less than half the fats and oils than our grandparents did and much fewer pulses, but more cereals and green vegetables. Today, curiously enough, bread, olive oil and tomatoes represent the same proportion of the total (cereals, fats and vegetables respectively) as they did in the 1920s. Our alimentary habits are growing closer to the northern model, but it is also true that we prefer our own produce over imported food. We are prepared to pay a lot more for a tomato from Sant Joan than one imported from Valencia, or for local beef or lamb over more renowned mainland meats.

It was from 1960 onwards that our diet began to change radically, for two reasons. On the one hand, the sudden prosperity provided by tourism and urban growth induced much of the agricultural population to abandon the poverty and hunger of a dying farm economy and to take jobs in construction and leisure. Their new urban status and purchasing power distanced them from their old customs, diet and culture. Tourism had arrived as the hardest years of the post-war period ended, a time of rationing and black market prices. The contrast between the two worlds is summed up in the ditty we used to sing at school:

> *Berigut, berigut*
> *figues seques amb pa aixut.*[1]

On the other hand, the hoteliers found themselves suddenly with thousands of summer visitors which had to be fed *a la europea*. There was little refrigerated transport at the time, so the local cattle business had to be bolstered. In Minorca, with its dairy tradition and lack of hotels, the

---

[1] Very good, very good,
Dried figs and stale bread.

cows outnumbered the tourists; but the Majorcan's traditional fat and protein came from olives and pork, so our meat and dairy production, such as it was, needed a shot in the arm to supply the holidaymakers with their butter, milk, beefsteaks and chicken. Of course, when the tourists went home for the winter, the production couldn't simply stop, so we islanders were cajoled into taking up the slack. We first had to be convinced that, in spite of the pink flab displayed by the northerners on the beaches, theirs was the Diet of Champions. Perhaps it was; in those years nobody would have prophesied that we'd eventually produce several decent basketball teams. Those were the heydays of Bimbo sliced bread, Laccao chocolate milk and the daily steak & chips.

In only a generation, kitchen habits also changed over to the northern model. Toss out the earthenware cooking pots and buy yourself a pressure-cooker! Empty the larder and stick a great big fridge in there! With the arrival of butane gas canisters, the old charcoal fireboxes disappeared from the kitchens of Palma, and with them the habit of toasting bread over the embers. Palma's air benefited, but the rural charcoal industry which supported many mountain families collapsed.

In the 1960s, a series of scientific studies, backed by a lot of facts and figures, claimed that the regular consumption of olive oil was harmful to human health. And we Spanish, so prone to believing in those days that everything home-grown must be inferior, fell for it hook, line and sinker. The new urban class started to buy the insipid, colourless imported soya and sunflower oils that began to flood the market at cheap prices. By the mid-seventies, there was no olive oil to be found in a cruet on any restaurant table (if indeed there was a cruet) but instead, some cute little curls of butter or margarine. Spain had always cultivated sunflowers because the salted seeds were a cheap and distracting snack (the shells could be dropped from the cinema balcony onto the expensive seats below), but now we began to produce enormous quantities of sunflower oil. A good part of the olive oil industry in the south had to be sold off at rock-bottom prices to Italian companies, and the Majorcan olive groves, once our greatest riches, were reduced to a hobby for those who could afford it. The dozens of small oil presses ground to a halt, the refinery closed down. But the world keeps turning and today we know it was a false alarm: the Phoenicians, Greeks and Romans were right all along. Virgin olive oil is one of the most complete foods available to humankind.

'Olive oil is a fat that has an especially healthy composition, which has been linked to a reduction of many kinds of illnesses, cancer among them' explains Dr Benito. 'There is a constant correlation between the intake of animal fats and cardio-vascular, cerebral and carcino-genic diseases. In relation to other countries, Spain and Greece are about halfway up the scale in terms of general consumption of oils and fat, so we should expect to have an average mortality rate, but ours is way below many other countries which consume lesser quantities of fat. That, above all, is because ours is mainly in the form of olive oil. Other factors and behavioural patterns are also a positive influence, but there's no doubt that there are good and bad fats. Among vegetable oils there are also some which are pernicious because they raise our cholesterol level, such as palm and coconut oil which are used a lot in the cake and biscuit industry. Saturated fats are, as a rule, those that solidify at room temperature: lard, butter, margarine, cocoa butter and coconut oil.'

Animal fats do contribute necessary elements to the human body, but should be consumed in moderation. They aren't recommended as a basic food because they increase the levels of 'pernicious' cholesterol (low density lipoprotein) in the blood. The plaques of LDL adhere to the walls of the arteries, obstructing the blood flow and impeding the proper irrigation of the body. High density lipoprotein, the so-called 'beneficial' cholesterol found in olive oil, acts as a drain-cleaner, sweeping the plaques of LDL along to the liver where they can be eliminated.

'The degree of acidity in olive oil has more effect upon one's palate and digestion than upon one's health. I personally love strong oil,' admits Dr Benito.

Sad to say, we've spent so many years consuming insipid substitutes that we've lost the habit of eating a really tasty oil.

And what can we say about pork? It's undeniably a part of the Christian Mediterranean diet, and the rituals of Martinmas slaughtering and sausage-making are an important part of our Balearic folk culture. Yet in our grandparents' day, not only were the pigs fed more healthily and bred in more humane conditions than today's porkers, the average rural family had to make one pig's worth of meat last all year round, which worked out to less than a tenth of the average ingestion of meat today.

'Pork has had a lot of bad press, but there isn't a clear case of it being bad for you, at least not when compared with beef,' says Dr Benito. 'The composition of pork fats has quite a lot in common with olive oil. There's a professor of biochemistry in the University of Saragossa, Professor Pocoví, who has come out in defence of pork by saying—tongue in cheek, of course—'We've come to the conclusion that the pig is essentially a four-legged olive."

Bon profit

Unlike the French, who wish you *bon appetit*, we Majorcans (perhaps less jaded and displaying a hearty appetite at all hours) wish our fellow diners *bon profit* or *que aprofiti*: may you make good use of what you eat.

The nutritive power of our food is important, but only in the measure that we can assimilate it. Our organism will absorb more iron from a slice of tomato than from swallowing a bag of nuts and bolts. To profit from the full nutritional value of the earth's bounties, it generally helps to eat them in their purest state whenever possible: raw (except some grains, cereals and tubers) and unrefined or unpeeled (the skin of the fruit or vegetables and the husk of the wheat or rice help the body to assimilate the vitamins and minerals). We absorb the full vitality of food when it is organically grown from unmanipulated seeds.

In order to digest raw dairy fats such as milk, butter, cream, etc, the intestine has to produce an enzyme called lactase to break them down and allow us to assimilate their high nutritional potential. Once weaned, we mammals stop producing lactase because we no longer need it; not even heifers drink milk once they're grown. However, as adults we can still get a lot out of dairy produce if it first loses the lactic sugar which makes it difficult for us to deal with. This is what happens to milk when turned into cheese, yoghurt or kefir.

The population of Holland has adapted over many generations to a diet rich in raw milk fats so most adult Dutch digestive systems still naturally produce lactase. The Minorcan dairy tradition has produced an adult population tolerant of raw milk, but most other Balearic adults prefer skimmed milk, yoghurt and cheese. In some parts of the world the majority of adults reject cow's milk outright. One of the first aid packages to the Orient, in the form of powdered milk, ended up doing a lot more harm than good.

A good number of the vitamins to be found naturally in milk and also in olive oil—E, A, D and K—are liposoluble; this means that the body can only assimilate them if they are dissolved in a fatty medium. If the milk is skimmed, these vitamins are as good as lost to us, and more have to be added to compensate. 'Added vitamin A, D and extra Calcium!' means basically, 'the natural vitamins we took out have been replaced with artificial ones'. The same goes for processed breakfast cereals 'fortified with 8 vitamins and iron!' Those they've have to add were the ones lost during the manufacturing process.

Our country, and the EU in general, produces more milk than it can sell. Do we Mediterraneans have to change our diet just to bail out the dairy industry? We're bombarded with adds urging adults to drink milk to combat osteoporosis, but who mentions the high choles-terol risk involved? Children and teenagers who are still growing can make use of the calcium content of milk, but what about adults, especially the typical Mediterranean types with a natural intolerance to milk? The Alimentary Guide of the Spanish and European Community Nutrition Society (funded, among others, by the dairy giant Danone) admits that, 'it doesn't appear that the calcium needs of this sector are any greater,' and 'it isn't certain that the intake of calcium is a key element in the maintenance of osseous mass'; in fact, it suggests, 'a high protein diet and excessive salt intake can be held accountable for the loss… of osseous mass.'

Olive oil contains vitamin D in a readily assimilated form; it is essential for our bones, and thus combats osteoporosis. An olive-oil rich diet also reduces the risk of breast cancer, which is provoked by an excess of saturated fats. Human mother's milk contains seven per cent of linoleic acid, a natural antioxidant; olive oil contains this same acid in exactly the same proportion. Could this be a key to the question of olive oil's excellent relationship with our organism? It may explain why a great deal of research is being carried out to create new oleaginous seeds capable of producing cheaper oils with this same characteristic.

A great deal of thought has been given to the subject of making the most of what we eat, and there are clearly good and bad combinations of foods. There are those which complement each other, helping the body to break each other down such as rice and beans, which are more nutritious together than apart; there are also those that give the body extra work when eaten together (see Dr Hay's famous Table of Incompatibilities). Needless to say, the ingredients of a basic bread & oil are, according to this table, perfectly compatible, although adding certain animal proteins is not!

One way of calculating how much our body gets out of the food it consumes, is to take note of the amount of energy or well-being it gives us in proportion to the effort needed to digest it. Another way is to take a peek at what's left over. Some European pigs are fed so many hormones and chemicals that their dung is too contaminated to use as manure and has to be treated as industrial waste: would ours also be considered as such? 'You are what you eat', but could we add, 'you're not what you excrete?' An old peasant who farms some land close to mine and passes the time of day complaining to me about this new-fangled

society, came up with this devastating condemnation:
'*Fins i tot, sa merda ja no fa olor a merda!*'[2]

Digestion

For food to be fully digested depends upon three things: it should be chewed properly before swallowing, contain plenty of fibre, and encounter a digestive system prepared to receive it.

The food served in a fast-food outlet is quick and easy to eat, requiring as much chewing as a marshmallow. This makes it very attractive for the young (for want of strong jaws) and old (for lack of molars). However, easy to eat often means hard to digest. A plate of brown bread & oil commands respect, and demands to be eaten at a more leisurely pace; it's quick to prepare but it can't be bolted down. One feels the need to enjoy the flavour and texture by eating it slowly, especially if the bread is consistent. But chewing isn't just grinding down; another important factor is salivation, what we're referring to when we say 'it makes my mouth water'. This, mixed with our food, aids the gastric juices in their work.

When I was a youngster, I appeared in a sketch filmed by my brother in Super-8, entitled 'The Hippie and the Bewitched *Pa amb Oli*' (our family obsession goes back a long way). The hippie in question stumbles upon the ingredients, prepares his bread and oil, and as he takes it to his mouth, it disappears thanks to clever editing. On watching the footage I was amazed to see myself so deep into my part that, while scrubbing the tomato on the bread my salivary glands could be seen to be working away like one of Pavlov's dogs. Over the years I have noticed that the

---

[2] 'Not even shit smells like shit anymore!'

simple act of preparing one's own bread & oil is a creative, sometimes quasi-religious ritual which provokes this salivary reaction, leading in turn to a satisfactory ingestion and digestion. Perhaps this preparative pause, so necessary for the proper assimilation of the coming meal, was the practical reason behind saying grace. What sensory stimulus can one expect from sticking a frozen lasagne in the microwave?

The second factor leading to good digestion is the presence of fibre in your diet. It is plentiful in your brown or whole-wheat bread, the tomatoes and the raw vegetables, olives and vinegar pickles. We don't make direct use of the fibre, but it regulates our digestive and bowel movements; put another way, it is the vehicle which allows the food's nutrients to be absorbed into the bloodstream. Meat (even the stringy variety) has hardly any fibre, nor do most processed foods.

'Vegetables and cereals are very easy for our body to assimilate', explains Dr Benito. 'For us to absorb animal protein, which is so similar to our own, our system has to make a great effort, straining our immune system, our defences. Eating meat every day, apart from being unnecessary, can put certain people at risk. All the research we have carried out upon this subject points to the fact that, not only is the Mediterranean-style diet very healthy for us, but it's about the healthiest in the Western world. The most long-living population group on the planet are Greek women, followed by Spanish women. Women are evidently the stronger sex—any view to the contrary is a lie invented by us men—but the life expectancy of Mediterranean men is much higher than in North Europe and North America, and the typical illnesses associated with the developed world rarer here than up north. It's not only our diet but our lifestyle which is healthier, but this is a subject which we've only recently begun to study, besides which it's difficult to measure or quantify.'

The habit of drinking wine and eating vinegar pickles with bread & oil is the third factor in the digestion question. They are secretagogues, which means that they stimulate the secretion of gastric juices, so when the main course reaches the belly the juices are ready to take care of business. Stimulating these secretions is also the purpose of the apéritif, another Mediterranean invention. Red wine, apart from this function of stimulating gastric secretion, has an important role as an antioxidant.

'An important study proved that those who drink one or two glasses of wine a day have a longer life expectancy than those who drink wine in excess, as well as those who don't drink at all,' says Dr Benito. 'That has been shown to be true. In moderate doses, wine can prevent cardio-vascular diseases: heart attacks and brain haemorrhages.' What about the teetotalling Moslems? Dr Mariné explains that the typical drink in the Arab world, green (unfermented) tea also contains polyphenols and other substances with antioxidant effects similar to those found in wine.

Olive oil itself also aids digestion because, as Lourdes March (one of our greatest authorities on the subject of oil) points out, 'it stimulates the gall-bladder, the bile flows better and our digestion benefits.' So, next time you're in a restaurant pondering over the menu, order the wine immediately and remember there's no harm in nibbling a few of those olives or a piece of that bread with some drops of oil and vinegar on it, even though when our kids do it, we snap, 'Stop that or you won't eat your supper!' The oil and vinegar stimulates the digestive system and that little bit of bread tempers our raging hunger, so when they take our order we can reconsider our initial urge to choose the *fava parada* (bean stew) followed by *porcella* (roast suckling pig).

Healthy recommendations

The aforementioned SENC publishes a Nutrition Guide for the Spanish Population in which we can find tips for a healthy diet, taking into account our regional, cultural and climatic differences.

As a rule, we are recommended to limit our intake of red and cured meats, sausages, sweets and pastries, etc to a few times a month; eggs, chicken, fish and pulses, a few times a week. Every day, the guide insists, we should eat cereals, vegetables or fruit; olive oil or dairy products; one or two glasses of wine (optional) and take part in some physical exercise. A long walk followed by bread & oil with tomato, accompanied by a glass of wine, cheese, and some raw fruit or vegetable (radish, apple, or green pepper which contains three times as much vitamin C per ounce as oranges) fits the bill perfectly.

If we accompany our bread and oil a few days a week with cheese, scrambled eggs, cold chicken or 'blue' fish (they contain a lot of calcium, magnesium, phosphorous, folic acid and B group vitamins), and occasionally splurge out on some ham or *camaiot*, we won't be contravening the SENC's recommendations. As for the question of fats, we read that we should:

—Diminish the intake of saturated fats which are present in meat products (animal fats), sweets and pastries (coconut and palm oil).
—Whenever our food budget allows it, we should choose and consume olive oil very

frequently, especially virgin olive oil, over and above sunflower or corn oil.

—Eat some 'blue' fish at least once a week because the oil contains omega-3 fatty acids which are physiologically important.

—Eating olives 'is a valid option, taking into account the healthy fats and other elements present'.

Teenage waistline

Dr José Mataix of the University of Granada, writes: 'The fatty-phobia which we find at street level can lead people to eliminate foods they consider being rich in fats, with the consequent loss of the energy that these fats contribute.'

Dr Marta Puig (pronounced 'pooch') is the author of a study of the nutritional habits of 421 students from fourteen to nineteen years of age living in Palma, and the only study I know which implicitly mentions bread & oil. According to Dr Puig, 'we are creating a generation of little Americans, with a clear tendency towards obesity. Television attacks on two flanks: the fact of sitting in front of the TV set induces one to eat snacks and not move, while the ads are constantly inciting us to buy processed foods, which nobody with a bit of common sense would otherwise pay good money for.' For every ad inviting the audience to consume real food such as olive oil or fruit, there are a hundred which try to convince it to buy 'healthy' products such as long-life dairy products, or sugared cereals 'with added vitamins'. I recall a study carried out in the UK some twenty years ago on a certain brand of breakfast cereals which came to the conclusion that the box attained almost the same nutritive value as its contents. But that was before manufacturers began to add the '8 vitamins'.

Dr Puig's study shows how the teenagers consume less

and less traditional food as they grow older and more responsible for their own feeding habits. The bread & oil option is represented in the questionnaire by the consumption of 'scrubbing tomatoes' and, of all the traditional dishes surveyed, it's the only one which holds up against the flood of foreign habits probably because any adolescent can make it himself. But the study also disclosed that a quarter of the students had never eaten bread & oil at home or anywhere else.

The pattern that emerges shows that as the adolescents become emancipated from parental dictates, they eat fewer traditional dishes and more fast food. Yet the average of fifteen monthly registers for bread & oil compares favourably with the four pizzas, three hamburgers and two hot dogs, and a lot better than the measly average one-and-a-half monthly registers for the traditional stuffed aubergines, stew, *tumbet*, *frit*, *cocarrois* and *panades*. In other words, *pa amb oli i tomàtiga* seems to be urban Majorcan youth's last link with their culinary heritage. The most bread & oil—an average twenty-four rations a month—is consumed by the youngest sector in this study, the fourteen-year-olds; perhaps they still listen to their mothers. The average drops to a dozen rations a month as the students reach sweet sixteen, when friends and fashion become the reference points. Girls between fourteen and nineteen, who perhaps have less freedom of movement than boys, maintain a higher fifteen rations a month.

The teenage tendency seems to be to eat bread & oil upon getting home at mid-afternoon or at suppertime. It is also fairly popular for elevenses—most school canteens prepare it—but not for breakfast or lunch. This suggests that the Mediterranean custom of lunch as the main meal of the day is still valid, whether at home or at school, and that each family member fixes himself a bread & oil-based light supper.

Of all the worries of adolescence, there are two related to diet, both aesthetic: pimples and flab. The fault for both lies much more with the sugars and saturated fats in fast or junk foods than with real bread or olive oil.

Dr Benito is scathing on this point: 'To convince us to eat fast food they have to resort to offering special deals or plastic toys. An adolescent will get more pimples from a hamburger than from a plate of bread & oil. From a nutritionist's or medical point of view it is important to note that our adolescents have jumped on the bandwagon of eating food which is completely foreign to our body needs. It's not just the food *per se*, it's the whole American Way of Life that goes with it. We ought to make young people see that our culture is several millennia old and the wisdom it encloses is a lot richer than the model that the communications media keep trying to sell us, but the media have the power and the money.

'The image which our young people have of themselves is completely distorted; thirty per cent of boys and sixty per cent of girls think they are fatter than they should be for their age and height, but when they are weighed and measured, only three per cent of the boys and five per cent of the girls turn out to be overweight. The model of physical perfection as projected by the media and the fashion industry is not what a healthy body should be. This leads to the pathologies of anorexia and bulimia which are the two extremes of this obsession. Our teenagers, under this influence, seem to have lost their own identity and are fixing their bearings upon an ideal which has nothing at all to do with what they really are.'

Dr Puig's study suggests that from the age of nineteen

onwards, Palma's youth begin to feel more responsible for their individual well-being, shedding their herd mentality and returning to local dietary patterns. This probably coincides with an awakening of their cultural identity, often kindled at university level. A recently published social study of Balearic youth draws a profile of our typical young islander as being politically liberal and with strong ecological tendencies. Many are conscious of the fact that the large-scale cattle breeding which supplies the fast-food chains represents a higher cost in natural resources than any other food fit for human consumption; the area of pasture needed to produce a pound of beef could produce cereals or vegetables of much higher nutritive value.

Dr Puig's study only covers the capital, which accounts for a quarter of the Balearic's population; results in the villages would probably be different due to lack of fast-food outlets and a more traditional family life. Nor do we know what happens to the over-twenties, but that is the age at which the body tends to begin to react to sustained bad alimentary habits and decides it's time to eat more healthily.

Denaturalized bread & oil

Not only are imported habits changing the face of bread & oil; local, national and EC regulations are beginning to stick their noses in where nobody asked them to. The water used for making the dough now has to be chlorinated, wood-fired ovens are tolerated but no new ones installed, neither wheat nor olives should be ground with stone mill-wheels, no oil over a certain degree of acidity should be sold, salt has to be refined, a small-scale farmer has to pay more in social security than he can get from selling his organic tomatoes.... All these restrictions are said to protect our health, but if this is really so it must be because we have created a race of human beings lacking in natural defences, weakened by an excess of sugars, antibiotics (taken directly or via animal meat) and other refined foods. We could paraphrase the dictum 'poetry is that which is lost in translation' by saying 'bread & oil's soul is to be found in that which doesn't meet the health regulations.'

The multinational fast-food chains have already begun attracting clients by offering regional variations. One day you'll be walking past the McDonalds next to the Bar Bosch and there on the menu in the window, right under the McChicken, you'll find McBread'noil, at which point you'll exclaim '*McAg en Dena*!'[3]

---

[3] '*Me cag en Dena*' A typical Majorcan oath, literally 'I shit on tens' (to avoid naming any deity as the recipient).

RECIPES

Recipes

BRINE

BOTTLING PRESERVES AND VINEGAR PICKLES

VINEGAR

EQUIPMENT

INGREDIENTS

OLIVES PANSIDES (WRINKLED OLIVES)

OLIVA VERDA TRENCADA (SPLIT GREEN OLIVES)

OLIVA VERDA SENCERA (WHOLE GREEN OLIVES)

OLIVA NEGRA O BLAVA (BLACK OR 'BLUE' OLIVES)

PICKLED SAMPHIRE

CAPERS

SUN-DRIED TOMATOES

PRESERVING IN OLIVE OIL: *ESCALIVADA*

FISH: ANCHOVIES AND SARDINES

EGGS

AROMATIC OILS

OLIVADA (BLACK OLIVE PASTE)

PESTO ALLO GENOVESE

MARTINMAS CHUTNEY

INSTANT CHUTNEY

HUMMUS

TUNA AND MAYONNAISE DIP

GUACAMOLE

AUBERGINE MOUSSE

SWEET AND SOUR CUCUMBER PICKLE

MISERIA

SWEET AND SOUR BEETROOT

PICKLED ONIONS

PICKLED ST. JOHN'S PEARS

One of the aims of this book is to point the reader down the path of self-sufficiency: fixing up a plate of bread & oil provides a satisfying feeling of direct participation in your own well-being. Money can buy you all the best ingredients, but if it's a question of spending, then spend some time in the kitchen, because nothing satisfies more than your own home-made accompaniments. Simply dressing a few *pansida* olives or marinating some fresh anchovies is well worth the effort, and closer to the spirit of *pa amb oli* than sending off for a Fortnum & Mason hamper.

I'm one of the secret fraternity of those who realize that the heart of any party is to be found in the kitchen. Let me encourage those of you who expect life to be served on a platter to get out of your armchair and into the pantry, get your fingers oily and enjoy the pleasure of discovering a world of pambossibilities. If you're holding back until The Three Kings bring you a Pambolinova set,[1] make yourself comfortable because you've a long wait ahead. Meanwhile, let me make some suggestions, all of them fairly cheap and simple. You don't have to go to the extreme of the Catalan chef Ferran Adrià of El Bulli de Roses (Girona), one of the best known in the country, who recently served a *sorbet de pa amb tomàquet* to the Spanish Minister of the Interior, challenging him to identify the taste. The aim here is not to raise the humble bread and oil to the spheres of *haute cuisine*, but to complement it with other honest and tasty recipes from the islands and beyond. Besides, a few recipes may help justify this book's presence in the cookery section of the bookshops.

---

[1] The British equivalent would be a Galt Toys 'Make Your Own Bread & Oil Kit'.

Basic Techniques

Brine

This is the basis for preparing green and black olives, and the first step in preparing many vinegar pickles such as capers, onions or samphire. To make up the brine, use a wide-necked stainless steel, glass or glazed ceramic container, and avoid any contact with cast iron, aluminium, etc. You should use pure sea-salt (without additives) and soft water, such as rainwater which has been collected off the roof (unfrequented by pigeons) and kept in the cistern. The spring water from the Tramuntana mountains tends to be quite hard due to the calcareous rocks through whose fissures it seeps underground. You will also need a clean, fresh hen's egg, which, like the water, should be at room temperature.

With enough water to cover the object of your pickling, add a spoonful of salt at a time, stirring with a wooden spoon or whisk until dissolved before adding the next, until you have a 10 per cent solution (100 grammes of salt per litre). To reach the optimum salinity of the brine, approximately 12 per cent of salt, some fine tuning is needed, and children can participate in and learn from the process. The egg is lowered into the water with a ladle, then more salt added and dissolved a teaspoon at a time, taking care not to crack the egg, until it begins to float. As the density of the brine nears that of the egg, this will rise to the surface and float like an iceberg. When the brine achieves the perfect pickling salinity—the minimum needed to preserve food—the egg's tide-mark will be about 2 cm in diameter. The egg is then removed and the brine ready.

Bottling preserves and vinegar pickles

The ideal containers are special glass preserving jars (Kilner jars) with renewable rubber sealing rings, but they can be expensive and come in very large sizes. At home, when we empty a jar of honey, mayonnaise or our home-made jam, we keep the glass jars whose screw-top lids are in good condition for bottling our own preserves and pickles. (Babyfood jars and plastic lids aren't reusable.) We soak the labels off and clean and dry them thoroughly, taking care not to damage the lids or scratch their thin rubber lining.

When preparing olives in brine, making the container airtight isn't necessary, but for most preserves it's fundamental, especially those containing sugar. For a good hermetic seal, the pot and lid should be sterilized by submerging them a few minutes in boiling water before filling them, to within half a centimetre of the top, with the warm produce. The lid is then screwed on tight and, upon cooling down, the half-centimetre of air contracts to form a vacuum which will keep the preserve in perfect condition at room temperature. Upon opening the jar, you will hear the characteristic 'pffft'. From then on, the jar should be kept in the fridge or in that proverbial cool, dry place: the larder.

Vinegar

It's important to buy good vinegar with a minimum acidity of 5°. For traditional Majorcan pickles, a quality wine vinegar is ideal, but I include recipes from northern cultures which do not share our wine-producing tradition and which use vinegars made of malt or even cider. Clear, distilled vinegars are more expensive and are used when it's important to maintain the colour of the contents, as in the case of pearl onions.

We Majorcans prefer our pickles sharp and just use pure vinegar, but when preparing samphire or capers, my northern genes sometimes prompt me to commit the sacrilege of steeping or dissolving herbs, spices and sugar in the vinegar first.

Equipment

One thing to keep in mind: always use stainless steel knives to slice lemons or to peel onions for pickling. Non-stainless steel pans, or enamel pans with a cracked or chipped surface, should be avoided when heating vinegar or acid fruit. Also avoid using earthenware *greixoneres* and aluminium, brass or copper pans when heating vinegar.

The traditional containers for keeping olives are the glazed pots (*alfàbies*) and large green glass jars (*barrals*) which are sometimes protected with canework. The lid usually consists of a cracked saucer which serves no other purpose. The canework and the dark green colour of the glass protect the olives from the pernicious effect of light. For reasons which become evident in the recipes for pickling olives, the shape of the pickling jar is important: whether it is amphora-shaped or cylindrical, it should narrow a little at the mouth.

To take the olives out of the container, take care not to use your fingers or a metal ladle; the ideal implement is the typical wooden ladle with holes in it, which drains the liquid back into the jar as you take out the olives, and usually comes with a hooked handle that allows it to be hung from the saucer-lid.

Ingredients

Many of the herbs or leaves mentioned are readily available in the Majorcan countryside, but take care not to pick any from the roadsides or ditches where the vegetation is yellowing or wilting: many local authorities find it cheaper to spray with weed-killer than use a strimmer. Also, the fact that somebody else's property is not fenced off may allow you right of way but not the right to pick anything you please. Organic products are available, but most small market gardeners who sell their own produce in the markets tend to go easy on the chemicals: just keep to what's in season and you won't go far wrong.

Indigenous recipes

Olives pansides (wrinkled olives)
Wrinkled olives
Virgin oil, salt
A few drops of lemon juice or vinegar
Crushed garlic, bay leaf, sweet paprika

Olives pansides can be found in the market from the beginning of October, either ready-dressed (at the pickles and dry fish stall) or straight from the olive grove at any greengrocer's. Given the chance, most of us prefer to prepare them to our own taste, as if dressing a salad. First rinse any dirt off the olives, put them in a salad bowl or earthenware *greixonera* and then add the above ingredients to taste. Mix them well and leave them for at least half an hour until they have absorbed the flavour of the condiments. I recommend you experiment with small quantities until you hit upon the combination that's right for you.

Oliva verda trencada (split green olives)

Green olives (enough to fill three-quarters of a large jar or pot)
More than enough brine to cover the olives
A good handful of fennel chopped into pieces
2 thick stems of fennel
(each a bit longer than the diameter of the mouth of the jar)
Fresh thyme
Fresh lemon leaves or carob leaves
Hot red peppers or chillies to taste

Green olives are picked directly off the tree in November, when they have attained their full size but not yet changed colour. The only time I've caught anybody stealing olives—they even brought their own ladder—they were green ones, which can fetch a high price in the market. Green olives can be pickled whole or split open. Now that we've entered the rat-race, split olives have become more popular because they can be eaten within a week of pickling whereas whole green olives are better from one year to the next. Splitting the olive allows the brine to penetrate quicker and 'kill' it, but for this same reason it doesn't keep as long.

The olives are first washed thoroughly (unless you can vouch for them being unsprayed) and split open by bashing each one once with a wooden mallet or a round stone. Wear an apron and do the job out of doors: the juice can splatter all over the kitchen, and if at first it's invisible it will soon turn into brown stains on your clothes and walls.

Divide the olives into four equal piles. Set aside the two long thick fennel stems, and divide the remaining dry ingredients (herbs, leaves and chillies) into five equal piles. You can also bash the thicker pieces of chopped fennel stems.

Wash the glazed ceramic *alfàbia* or glass *barral* thoroughly and place a layer of the herbs and leaves on the bottom. Take the first pile of olives and spread it over the condiments and proceed, alternating layers until you reach the point in which the jar narrows, finishing off with a layer of herbs and leaves.

The stems of fennel are used to stop the rest of the ingredients floating to the surface when the brine is poured over them. Take a stem of fennel and bend it until it fits through the mouth of the jar, then release it so it springs back into place across the top layer. Do the same with the other stem, placing it at right angles to the first. Pour the brine over the olives and condiments until they are covered, then place a saucer over the mouth, which will stop insects getting in but allow any gas produced by the maturing process to escape.

Oliva verda sencera (whole green olives)

The process is the same as for split olives, but some people leave the olives in pure water for a few days, changing it a couple of times, before putting them in brine. This helps get rid of excess bitterness in the olives. Once the jar is filled with alternating layers of olives and condiments and held down by the fennel sticks, pour on the brine allowing a little extra to account for evaporation, and cover. These olives need at least six months to mature, although they are better if you wait a whole year. Place them in a corner of the larder where they won't have to be moved.

When the saucer is finally lifted, it might reveal a disgusting mouldy scum on the surface of the brine. Don't panic or pour the whole thing down the toilet; simply remove the scum with care and the olives underneath should be perfectly all right.

Oliva negra o blava
(black or 'blue' olives)

'Blue' olives
Rain water
Vinegar
Garlic, bay leaf
Virgin olive oil, salt

The last Majorcan olives to ripen on the tree, those which missed the last trip to the oil press and yet were spared by the thrushes, aren't really black but more of an indigo colour. Some people prepare them the same way as whole green olives, although there's no need to soak them first to get rid of the bitterness; nor do they keep quite as long. This is how Na Fiola, the baker, prepares them:

'Wash the olives and place them in a clean *alfàbia*. For every kilo of olives add four cloves of garlic, two bay leaves and two coffee spoons of salt. Prepare a mixture of two parts vinegar to three of water and pour it over the olives until they are covered. Add a dash of virgin olive oil (to keep the flavour in and the microbes out) and leave them, covered with a saucer, for at least month.' The olives will be an intense black colour.

Pickled samphire

Samphire
Brine
Vinegar

All wild plants in the Balearic Islands are protected by law, which is normally only applied in cases of flagrant abuse, such as putting the plant's life or your own in danger. Nobody will probably object to your gathering a few wild asparagus for an omelette, nor a handful or two of tender samphire sprigs; just go easy, don't pull up the roots, damage the stems or pick them by the basketful.

Around the June equinox, the samphire begins to sprout new shoots, which are the best for pickling; some should always be left on the plant, to ensure its survival. The leaves and stems snap easily, so before stuffing the sprigs tightly into glass jars leave them to wilt for a day or two; they will pack better without breaking, and recuperate their terseness.

Thanks to its coastal habitat, samphire is already quite salty, so it will only need a couple of hours in brine before being drained and the water replaced by vinegar. If the jars are hermetically sealed, the samphire will keep for at least a year. When the first strings of tomatoes hit the market in late September, your equinoctial samphire will be ready to accompany the first scrubbed-tomato bread & oil of the autumn.

Capers

Capers
Brine
Vinegar

Caper bushes grow low to the ground, often more than two metres in diameter, with long trailing stems along which the caper buds appear. They are typical of the Mediterranean and grow wild near the coast, but here they are cultivated as far inland as the sea breeze reaches. In summer, they are the vivid green smudges visible on the parched yellow fields from Llubí to Campos. In plant nurseries or in the market you will find caper bushes ready to transplant; they need little water but a deep, well drained soil. In May they begin to produce delicately perfumed white orchid-like flowers which wilt after a day. Every flower in bloom is a caper less because the *tapera* itself is the tiny bud; the smaller it is picked, the more exquisite the taste, the higher the price, and the more are needed to fill a jar. Once they begin to swell prior to flowering and will no longer pass through a special measuring sieve, they are known as *taperots* and fetch a third of the price. The plant has to be visited regularly because the thorny shoots grow rapidly, producing buds and then flowers as they trail along the ground. Once wilted, the flower gives way to the caper berry, known as the *cavall*, which resembles a gooseberry with a stalk at either end, and can also be pickled. You'll find them ready to eat at the olive and pickles stalls. In Campos, the tender end of the shoot is also pickled, before the thorns have formed and while the leaves are still a little fluffy.

To pickle small capers, leave them two days in brine (the *taperots* and *cavalls* need longer) before draining and bottling them in vinegar for six weeks. Use small airtight mustard jars; capers are consumed slowly. In large jars, once open, they may spoil.

Sun-dried tomatoes

Tomatoes
Salt
Sunshine

Choose ripe summer tomatoes that are flatter rather than spherical, wash them and while still damp, roll them in a plate of salt. Slice them horizontally and then sprinkle the slice with salt. In a well aired, sunny spot, leave them out to dry, cut side upwards, on a cane or wicker tray or wire rack, taking care to bring them indoors before the *serena* or evening dew falls. Once they have lost ninety-five per cent of their original weight and are as flat as a mat (about four or five days), they can be sewn onto strings to be kept in the pantry. Another option is to brush off some of the excess salt, place them in glass jars, and cover them with olive oil along with some fresh basil and crushed garlic.

Most of the work boils down to taking them indoors at night, so it's worthwhile preparing a lot at a time, especially when tomatoes are cheap. Don't forget that you'll need twenty kilos of fresh tomatoes to produce one of dried, but then the flavour is so intense that half a dried tomato is more than enough to accompany a plate of bread & oil, and can be considered the vegetarian equivalent of cured ham.

Preserving in olive oil

Apart from sun-dried tomatoes and cheese, there are many foods that can be kept in olive oil: tuna fish, sardines and roast vegetables, but the process may be a bit too complicated to go into here. I'll stick to the Catalan *escalivada* which is more of a sweet pepper and aubergine salad than a preserve. It goes very well with our bread & oil because the vegetables are cut into strips which fit the elongated slices of Majorcan bread to a tee. If the *escalivada* is still warm and served on toasted bread & oil, the effect is magnificent.

2 aubergines
4 sweet red peppers
(best if they are in the process of
turning colour from green to red)
1 clove of garlic (or more, to taste)
1/2 glass (125 ml) of virgin olive oil, salt

Crush the garlic in the mortar, adding the oil a bit at a time until it becomes a paste. Then pour in the rest of the oil, mix, and reserve. Prick the aubergines with a fork so they don't explode, and roast them with the red peppers, whole and unpeeled, over hot coals. Turn them regularly so they cook evenly, until they are soft and well cooked inside; the skin of the peppers will be black and blistered, but this doesn't affect the flesh. They can also be roasted on the rack of a hot oven, but won't achieve the same smoky taste. Put them in a covered bowl and wait until they have cooled down enough to handle. Remove the stalks and seeds from the peppers, letting the liquid drain back into the bowl. Peel them and cut or tear the flesh into finger-sized strips, putting them in a serving dish, doing the same with the aubergines. Strain the red pepper juice from the first bowl into the olive oil and mix well. Pour all the liquid over the strips of pepper and aubergine, add salt to taste and stir. Eat while still warm, with your bread & oil. This dish will keep for a week in the fridge.

Fish

The anchovies we are used to eating are cured in a special way, in brine with part of their own blood, which accounts for the reddish-brown colour. What we know as *seitons* (in Spanish, *boquerones*) are the same fish left to marinate in vinegar, which explains why they're white.

Xisca Soler tells me how to marinate anchovies. 'Before buying them ready-made, think how easy it is to prepare them yourself; there's no shortage of local anchovies in the fish market. You take off the head, pulling towards the tail, and the innards come with it; then with one finger, you lift off the spine. Then you rinse the fish, and leave them overnight in vinegar. The next day you sprinkle a bit of chopped parsley and garlic over them, with a dash of olive oil, and they're ready to complement your bread & oil, especially when accompanied with some strips of roast sweet pepper.'

Jordi Ramone, drummer with the Pa Amb Oli Band and captain of a fishing boat, prepares marinated sardines like this:

1 kg fresh sardines
Flour for coating
1 litre vinegar
250 ml water
1 large white Majorcan onion
Bay leaves, salt,
Olive oil for frying

'Clean a kilo of fresh sardines, salt them, dip them in flour and fry them lightly in olive oil. Drain them of oil and place them in a pot or an earthenware *greixonera*—just make sure not to use an iron pan. Now cut a white onion into thin crescent slices and sauté them in olive oil until they begin to turn colour at the points. Put two bay leaves in the pan and add four glasses (a litre) of vinegar and one of water, letting it come to the boil for a minute to absorb the flavour of the bay leaves. When it has cooled down, pour the contents of the pan over the sardines and leave them to marinate. After four days in the fridge or the larder they're ready to eat with your bread & oil.'

Eggs

A toasted bread & oil with eggs is a complete light supper. Scrambled eggs with freshly ground pepper are delicious, but the French omelette is a classic and can be made to fit the slice of toast. We don't add milk to either omelettes or scrambled eggs but otherwise the technique is the same.

Here are some popular local variations on the theme; just add the following ingredients to the beaten eggs:

• Fresh chopped herbs: parsley, basil, chives, marjoram or oregano.
• White Majorcan onion (100 grammes per egg) cut into thin slices and sautéed over a low heat until transparent but juicy, then dried on kitchen paper.
• Vegetables: often you come back from a country ramble with half-a-dozen asparagus shoots, or a couple of edible mushrooms, which aren't enough to make up a full dish but give a boost to an individual omelette. Sauté them for five minutes with chopped garlic and parsley before adding them to the eggs. Try also using tender fava beans and spring onion or garlic shoots.
• To make a cheese or tuna omelette, sprinkle the grated cheese or the flakes of tuna onto the omelette as it's cooking and before folding it over.
• Chopped hard-boiled or pickled eggs are also delicious with bread & oil; to stop them falling off the slice, mash them first with a drop of vinegar or white wine.

Imported recipes

Aromatic oils
We've all seen oil cruets with a clove of garlic or a red pepper inside, but the habit of spicing or flavouring oils and vinegars is more common in France than here. Depending upon the herbs used, the oil will be an appropriate complement to a salad, meat, fish or bread & oil. It's a good way to bestow some character upon a fine

but insipid oil, which doesn't tend to be our case here in the Islands. However, if you want to try, the technique is simple. In a mortar, crush a handful of aromatic herbs, which should be rinsed clean of dirt, but not wet. Basil, rosemary, oregano and marjoram all work well, individually or in different combinations; you can add crushed garlic or spices. In a sterilized glass jar, place a layer of herbs, sprinkle some salt over them and repeat the process until the jar is three-quarters full. Extra Virgin oil is poured over until it covers the herbs and the pot is covered tightly and set upon the window-sill in the full sunlight. After three weeks (depending upon the weather) it will have absorbed the flavour and other properties of the herbs. The oil is filtered through a cloth and decanted to a clean bottle or cruet.

Condiments and sauces

At home we've picked up the habit of always having some sauce or pickle on the bread & oil table; if it's concentrated, a coffee-spoonful is enough to make it rock. Sometimes we buy the sweet Swedish mustard which they make and sell at the *Svarta Pannan* restaurant behind the Bar Bosch. At any delicatessen you'll find chutney, pesto or *olivada*, but to make it yourself isn't that difficult, and you can keep it all year round.

Olivada (black olive paste)

We've always had a lot of contact with Italy but we've never learned their trick of turning black olives into a condiment. The Catalans have discovered this lucrative outlet for their quality black olives, selling the paste in expensive little jars under the name of *Olivó* or *Olivada*, but as far as I can tell, this isn't a deeply rooted tradition in

Catalonia either. Olive paste is also now being made on the island, and is bought mainly by foreigners who eat it with fish and other Mediterranean dishes. It's great on bread & oil.

Pansida *olives*
(or black canned stoneless olives if it is for keeping)
Virgin or Extra Virgin olive oil
Salt

Half the work is removing the stones from the olives; this is easy when you have a cherry-stoning device. Pass the stoned olives through a fine Mouli sieve to leave the skins behind, then add oil to the purée and salt to taste. (If using tinned olives, you can add a bit of the liquid.) Fill small mustard size glass jars with the paste to within a centimetre of the lid, top up with more oil and then seal.

Pesto allo Genovese

I've heard that the village of Gènova was founded by Genovese fishermen who, being foreigners, weren't allowed to reside within Palma's city walls. If this is so, they didn't leave us this recipe, although all the ingredients are well known to us. Pesto is usually eaten with pasta or *gnocchi*, but will bring a summer flavour to a winter *pa amb oli*.

A generous handful about 45 g chopped basil with some parsley
12 blanched almonds or the equivalent ground almonds
*2 teaspoons pine nuts (*pinyons)
1 clove of garlic, crushed
100 ml extra virgin or virgin oil
100 g very finely grated cheese

(ideally Asiago and Romano in equal parts,
but Parmesan will do)
Some drops of lemon juice (optional)
Salt to taste

The name comes from the pestle which is used to crush the ingredients in the mortar, but if you're in a hurry you can put the whole lot through the blender until you get a smooth paste. If you wish to keep it, fill pots as in the last recipe.

If you use it with your pasta, set aside a soup-spoon per person of the cooking water with which to dilute the pesto.

Martinmas chutney

Chutney can be made of many different fruits and vegetables, but not everything works. Ideally you should use mango, but apricots, peaches, pears, pumpkin, apple and even loquats (*nispros*) can produce a good chutney. Around Martinmas, when the cold begins and the last tomatoes in the garden don't seem to ripen, they can be turned into this chutney, which I recommend with bread & oil and cheese. This recipe makes about 8 to 10 one-pound pots. Before starting, make sure your kitchen is well ventilated.

1.5 kg green tomatoes, cut into thin slices
*500 g peeled, cored and chopped cooking apple (*poma àcida)
500 g chopped onion
250 g seedless raisins or sultanas
250 g brown sugar
15 g salt
15 g finely minced fresh ginger root or

¹/₂ teaspoon ground ginger
375 ml vinegar (malt if possible)
1 coffee spoon of pebrebò coent *(hot ground paprika)*
1 teaspoon mustard or ¹/₂ teaspoon mustard powder
(Other spices can be added:
ground cinnamon, cloves or coriander)

Put all the ingredients in a large (4 litre) enamel or stainless steel pan, bring gradually to the boil stirring all the while until the sugar has dissolved. Lower the flame and simmer, stirring occasionally, until the chutney has begun to thicken and is fairly homogenous, which will take about an hour. Meanwhile, sterilize the pots for a minute in boiling water. Pour or ladle the chutney into the warm pots and seal. It's best left to mature until Christmas.

Instant chutney

For an impromptu *pa amb oli à deux*, or while waiting for the previous recipe to mature, you can fall back on this false chutney. Take four tablespoons of apricot or peach jam, add a few drops of vinegar and as many of Worcestershire sauce, a pinch of salt and another of your favourite spice (curry powder, ground ginger, coriander), stir it up and *uep!* There you have it.

Dips

As you like it: dip a corner of your slice, cut it into strips first, or spoon some onto your plate. You can also dip Inca biscuits (oiled and tomatoed), raw vegetables or potato crisps into these sauces.

Hummus

Pulses are an important part of the Mediterranean diet, yet it seems nobody has time for them anymore. I know of two ways to eat them with bread & oil; committing sacrilege (baked beans on oiled toast) or making hummus as the eastern Mediterraneans do.

*500 g of cooked chickpeas (*ciurons*) passed through a mouli*
200 ml virgin or extra virgin olive oil
The juice of a fresh lemon, or to taste
2 tablespoons of tahini *(sesame paste)*
1–2 cloves (to taste) of garlic, crushed
Salt
*Sweet ground paprika (*prebebò*) and black olives to decorate*

Begin by making a purée of the cooked chickpeas. You can put them through the blender, but using a mouli sieve you will eliminate the skins which are responsible for chickpeas' flatulent reputation. *Tahini* is rare in Spain, except for the expensive organic variety sold at health shops. You can make it by crushing sesame seeds in the mortar or whizzing in an electric blender and adding a few drops of water until it emulsifies like mayonnaise.

Mix the chickpea purée and *tahini* with the oil in a bowl, adding the lemon juice and salt, to taste. You can then add water to make the hummus a bit lighter. When you have reached the desired consistency, transfer to a serving dish, sprinkle some sweet paprika over the surface and decorate with black olives. Finish with a flourish of olive oil from the *setrill*, which prevents it from drying out if kept in the fridge (two or three days).

Tuna and mayonnaise

This is very popular with kids.

A small pot of mayonnaise (125 g)
A small tin of tuna fish in oil (80 g)
A few drops of lemon juice

The ingredients are simply mashed together or put through the blender. But the basic recipe lends itself to all kinds of variations by simply adding fresh herbs, garlic, spices or chopped hard-boiled egg with a dash of ketchup and Worcestershire sauce.

Guacamole

A tex-mex *pa amb oli*? Plenty of calories for the cold, damp Majorcan winters. If you can, buy local avocados which are available from November to March. They may be smaller than their tropical cousins but the flesh is smooth as butter and very tasty, not having had to be refrigerated.

The authentic Mexican touch comes from fresh lime juice and finely chopped coriander leaves; both are difficult to find in Majorcan shops, but in my orchard I can grow all the fresh ingredients for my guacamole.

2–3 ripe avocados
2 teaspoons finely chopped fresh coriander or
half of powdered coriander
1 small white onion or the whites of
2 spring onions, finely chopped
The juice of a lime or lemon
3 tablespoons virgin olive oil
1 medium-sized tomato, chopped (skinned and seeds removed)
Salt, Worcestershire sauce and Tabasco to taste

Cut the avocados in four vertically, remove the stones and set them aside. The skin can be peeled back easily and the pulp placed in a bowl, mashed with the oil and half the lime or lemon juice until a smooth paste is formed; this can be done with a blender. The chopped onion, coriander and tomato are stirred in and the other ingredients (including the remaining juice) added gradually, to taste. Put one or both of the stones in the guacamole to keep it from turning greyish-brown until it is eaten. In an airtight container in the larder it will keep a day or two, or a week in the refrigerator. It is particularly good with oil-and-tomatoed Inca biscuits.

Aubergine mousse

This is an adaptation of a side dish which is popular in the Middle East, from the Lebanon to Iran. It is best made earlier in the aubergine season, before October when they become full of seeds and sometimes even spicy.

500 g aubergines
1 pot ('Greek' or 'Bulgarian' style) thick yoghurt (125 g)
2 or 3 cloves of garlic, minced or crushed
1/2 bunch parsley, chopped (two tablespoons)
1/2 teaspoon ground cinnamon
1/2 teaspoon curry powder (optional)
Salt to taste

First, the aubergine must be softened by cooking. There are three basic ways, each giving a slightly different flavour:

A. Roast the whole aubergine in the oven or over the embers until it is soft, then peel.

B. Peeled and diced, steam for 10 minutes.

C. Peeled and diced, put them, lightly salted, in a

colander; after half an hour they have begun to 'sweat'. Squeeze the liquid out of the diced aubergines a handful at a time and sauté slowly in olive oil until soft.

Once cooked, put the aubergine with the other ingredients (except the yoghurt) through the blender or mouli sieve. Now we add the yoghurt and stir it in with a fork. Add salt to taste and eat warm or cold.

Sweet pickles and
other northern barbarities

Our Northern visitors may be barbarians in their speech, dress and manners, but not all their culinary habits are barbarisms. You've heard of blue-eyed soul: here are some ideas for a blue-eyed bread 'n oil.

Sweet and sour cucumber

250 g cucumbers
(the best are small, young and firm,
with few seeds and a prickly skin)
Salt
5 tablespoons good wine or malt vinegar
2 tablespoons (to taste) brown or white sugar
1 teaspoon chopped fresh or dried dill

Before peeling the cucumber, some of the bitterness can be eliminated by slicing off the top and scrubbing it across the cut. It will begin to froth a bit; this is the bitter juice leaving. Peel off a few strips of the skin, leaving the cucumber striped, and slice it into thin rounds. Place them in a colander, salt them well, and leave to stand. Meanwhile, put the other ingredients into a clean screw-top jar, and shake vigorously until the sugar is dissolved. Now squeeze the water out of the cucumber slices with your hands and place them in the jar; close and shake it again, then leave for a couple of hours before eating. They will keep for a few days in this way. If you wish to store the cucumber for a longer time, the jars should be sterilized and the vinegar, sugar and spices brought to the boil and then cooled before introducing the cucumber.

Miseria

This is an adaptation of a standard Polish side dish, cucumber in yoghurt. It's very refreshing when eaten cool.

250 g young cucumbers
1 pot yoghurt or crème fraîche (125 g)
1 teaspoon chopped fresh or dried dill
Lemon juice (optional) to taste
Salt

Proceed with slicing, scrubbing, peeling, salting and squeezing the cucumber as in the previous recipe. Place it in a bowl and mix in the other ingredients. A Turkish variation replaces the dill with chopped fresh fennel shoots and mint, crushed garlic and a teaspoon of olive oil before adding the yoghurt.

Either of these two variations can be sent through the blender, with water, to make a refreshing cold summer soup.

Sweet and sour beetroot

A bunch of beetroots at a market stall looks very tempting, but it's mainly the foreigners who buy them because we don't know the culinary possibilities of this rich source of iron.

Use rubber gloves for peeling and slicing them, to avoid

ending up with scarlet fingers. They are very healthy eaten raw, simply peeled and grated, but in small quantities; the next morning you may find your urine red! I know of someone who checked in for a whole series of clinical tests before he remembered that he had eaten beetroot the night before.

The following is a way of eating them in small doses.

1 bunch of beetroots (about 300 g when peeled) sliced
3 tablespoons vinegar
2 tablespoons sugar (white or brown)
1 teaspoon salt
1 teaspoon cumin seeds

Peel the beetroots, cut them in half and then into thin slices. Put them in a small stainless steel saucepan with the other ingredients and then add enough water to cover. Bring slowly to the boil, stirring occasionally, then simmer, covered, for about fifteen minutes, adding more water if the liquid evaporates. They can be bottled in a sterilized airtight jar for keeping, or served as soon as they've cooled down; in a bowl they will keep several days in the fridge.

Pickled onions

The nearest British equivalent to our *pa amb oli*, conceptually and socially, is a ploughman's lunch, which is nearly always served with these sweet-and-sour pickles, larger and darker than our pearl onions. If it wasn't for the bother of peeling them, they'd be very easy to prepare. I make a whole batch as soon as they appear in the market in October, and we've polished them off before Christmas. Now that you can buy Cheddar cheese in most Majorcan supermarkets, make some pickled onions and enjoy a ploughman's *pa amb oli.*

500 g small onions or shallots
Brine
Approximately 300 ml vinegar (malt is best)
Approximately 100 g brown sugar
Whole spices: cloves, bay leaves, slices of ginger root, cinnamon
stick, cardamom pods, peppercorns

The onions or shallots are peeled (easier said than done) with a stainless steel knife and left overnight in a stainless or enamel saucepan of brine, with a saucer on top of them to keep them submerged. If you can find any ready-peeled onions, you'll have saved all the hard part!

The next day, sterilize some glass jars and let them cool. Drain the onions, keeping the empty saucepan handy. Pack the onions into the jars, firmly but without squashing, then top them up with vinegar. Taking care not to let the onions fall out, pour the vinegar out of the jars and into the saucepan. Add sugar; at home we prefer a ratio of one part of sugar to three of vinegar. Now, for each pot of onions, add to the saucepan the following spices: one bay leaf, one whole clove, a centimetre of cinnamon stick and a slice of root ginger and a few peppercorns and mustard seeds. Bring the vinegar to the boil, making sure the sugar has dissolved, cover and let it cool to blood temperature. Distribute the spices equally among the jars and top them up with the warm sweet vinegar. If it's too hot, the onions will lose their crispness; if too cold, they won't keep as well. Cover and seal, then leave the onions to mature for at least two weeks before eating with your bread & oil. The leftover spiced vinegar can be used in salad dressings.

Pickled St John's pears

Another British recipe adapted to our latitudes. Our small, firm *peres de Sant Joan*, which ripen around the summer solstice, are ideal for this purpose.

1 kg peres de Sant Joan *or other firm-fleshed pears*
500 g sugar
250 ml vinegar (distilled malt vinegar would be best)
A strip of fresh lemon peel
A whole clove for each pear
A few slivers of fresh ginger
1/2 cinnamon stick
1/2 teaspoon salt

Peel the *peres de Sant Joan*, leaving the stalk. If using larger pears, peel, core and cut them into slices.

Heat the sugar, spices and vinegar in a stainless steel or enamel saucepan, stirring until the sugar has dissolved. Add the pears, cover and simmer for about twenty minutes or until they are tender. Meanwhile, sterilize the jars. Lift the pears out of the saucepan and pack them tightly into the warm jars. If they are whole, leave at least one stalk uppermost! Let the syrup simmer another ten minutes to thicken and pour through a strainer over the pears. Cover and seal the jars, put them in the larder and forget about them until Boxing Day, when you can eat your pickled pears with bread & oil and cold turkey.

THE OILY PAGES

The Oily Pages

A *pa amb oli* guide to Majorca

*'Man cannot live by bread alone;
he needs a trickle of oil and a pinch of salt.'*

There is no census of traditional bakeries, directory of *pa amb oli* cafés or any other information related to the Majorcan bread & oil scene so I have gathered this information as best I could. Since the original edition of this book came out, I've tried to keep it up to date.

Traditional Bakeries
still using wood-fired ovens

Alaró *Ca Na Juanaineta* (Carrer d'en Mig, 24)
Algaida *Can Salen* (Laberint, 16)
Andratx *Forn de s'Hostal* (Libertad, 38)
Calonge (Santanyí) *Forn Adrover* (Rafel Adrover, 5)
Campos *Can Vadell* (Manacor, 19)
    Can Pere (Fray Francisco Javier Ballester, 11)
Consell *Forn de sa Plaça* (Rector Munar, 2)
Palma *Pastelería La Deliciosa* (Blanquerna, 15)

Forn des Paners (Paners, 7)

Forn de Sa Pelleteria (C. Pelleteria)

Forn de la Pau (Carrer de la Pau, 12)

Forn Cremat (Can Cavallería, 15B)

Forn Fondo (Unió, 15)

Forn de Sant Elies (Sant Elies, 8 off Carrer dels Oms)

Forn de La Glòria (Carrer del Forn de la Glòria, 9)

Pepi (Concha Espina 23, La Vileta)

Can Guiem (C/ València, 1, Secar de La Real)

Forn de sa Garriga (Camí Destre, 50, Son Sardina)

Pollença *Can Nas* (Plaça Vella)

Can Porgador (Carrer de l'Horta)

Petra *Can Jaume* (Pare Palou, 1)

Santanyi *Forn de s'Aljub* (Carrer de s'Aljub, 1)

Can Gelat (Centro, 24)

Sineu *Can Pinara* (Esperança, 15)

Can Guillemet, a.k.a. *Forn de sa Plaça* (on the main
    square)

Valldemossa *Can Molinas* (Bakeries at Rei Sanxo, 3 and
    Carrer de la Rosa, 4; shop at Blanquerna 15)

Flour Mills

Sineu *Amador Camps* (Tel. 971 52 00 17)

Montuïri *Harinas Gomila* (Mestre Porcel, 29. Tel 646006)

Other Ingredients

Cured meats and cheeses are usually sold in the *xarcuteria*
(delicatessen) counters at supermarkets and stalls in the
market-places in larger towns or weekly village markets.
There are some excellent but expensive *colmados* in Palma
where you can find the choicest local meats, cheeses, patés,
pickles, oils and wines:

La Pajarita (Sant Nicolau, 4)
La Favorita (Sant Miquel,38)
La Montaña (Jaume II, 27)
Son Vivot (Sa Porta Pintada 1, off Plaça Espanya)
La Luna (Oms, 3)
Colmado Santo Domingo (Costa de Santo Domingo)
Can Manresa (Fàbrica 19, near Sta Catalina market)
Club del Gourmet, El Corte Inglés (Jaume III)

Olive Oil

Local virgin oils can be bought in most good groceries and
supermarkets:

Oli d'Oliva Verge Caimari (Majorcan virgin oil from
Caimari and the pla)
Verge Extra Antoni Mateu (Majorcan extra virgin oil from
Caimari and the pla)
Oli Can Det (Sóller Virgin oil)
Olis Sóller (Sóller Extra Virgin oil)
Oli Solivelles (Extra Virgin from Alcudia)
Aubocassa (highly rated Extra Virgin Arbequina oil from
Manacor)

Other local virgin oils mixed with mainland oils to bring
down their acidity include *Olis Sóller's* '*Sa Tafona*' and *Olis
Martorell's* '*Gust d'Oliva*'.

Local Wines

D.O. Binissalem (Binissalem, Consell, Sta Maria, Sencelles)
Albaflor (Jaume Nadal, Binissalem)
The classic *Binissalem Auténtico* and the young *Binissalem*

Jove are bottled by José L. Ferrer, Binissalem

Macià Batle (Macià Batle, Sta Maria)

Hereus de Ribas (Hereus de Ribas, Consell, one of the oldest bodegas on the island)

Jaume de Puntiró (Sta Maria) bottles two good organic red wines, Vermell and Carmesí.

Son Campaner is an excellent new red (Tramontana Solar, Sencelles)

D.O. Pla i Llevant (Porreres, Manacor, Algaida, Petra, Felanitx)

L'Arxiduc, Mossèn, Pere Seda (Pere Seda, Manacor)

Mont Ferrutx, Ses Ferritges, Aia (Miquel Oliver, Petra)

Butibalusí (organic) Can Majoral (Can Majoral, Algaida)

Ànima Negre, AN2 (Ànima Negre, Felanitx)—a highly regarded red.

Gall Vermell, Jaume Mesquida, Maria Esther (Jaume Mesquida, Porreres, who also produces Majorca's first Brut Nature dry sparkling wine).

Vi de la Terra, soon to be known as D.O. Serra de Tramuntana (north and south slopes of the Serra, from Andratx to Alcudia)

Stairway to Heaven (Castell Miquel, Alaró)

Son Puig (Son Puig, Puigpunyent)

Ambrat (Estellencs) and *Cornet* (Banyalbufar) are two dry white Malvasia wines; these vineyards have been reintroduced to the area which made them famous a century ago.

Santa Catarina (Santa Catarina, Andratx) the first bodega to make Majorcan wines for export, with vineyards in the Pla i Llevant area as well as Andratx.

Salt

The salt flats around Es Trenc now produce the excellent *Flor de Sal d'Es Trenc*, a *fleur de sel* harvested by hand. It can be found locally in gourmet shops in various flavours: white (normal), pink (hibiscus flavour), black (olives) and green (Mediterranean herbs) and is also exported world-wide.

Cheeses

It's worth seeking out the excellent goat-and-sheep cheese, both fresh and cured, made by S'Atalaia in Llucmajor. Other well-known local cheeses are the goat's cheese from Cas Concos and the well known *Formatges Piris* in Campos and Can Montes near s'Arenal.

There are dozens of small producers of farmhouse *maonès*, the excellent Minorcan cheese, sold in the better *xarcuterias*.

Traditional cured meats

Mateu Putxer makes his specialities at Matanza Mallorquina Artesana (Muntanya 39, Sa Pobla) and they are carried by the better shops.

A different, but respectable, outfit is Cas Putxer (Aurora 7, Binissalem).

Can Rafel (Sta Catalina, 20, Artá) makes traditional farmhouse meats.

There are two good traditional pâté manufacturers in Sóller, the classic La Luna (Av. d'Asturies, 4) and the more adventurous Can Matarino (Camí de Biniaraix,17).

The Minorcan *carn i xuia* can be found in Can Vivot.

Pickles

Many people say the best capers are bottled by the co-operative in Llubí (Carrer de Sineu, 41) under the name *Sa Llubinera*. They also prepare samphire, olives, etc which can be found in Palma at La Favorita.

Other local picklers are *Conservas Rosselló* and *Olives Caimari*. In the markets, you will find pickle stalls which also sell salted fish.

Where to eat it

Many Majorcan restaurants and cellers also offer *pa amb oli* as a first course and most village cafés or Palma bars will make you one if asked, although they might not include virgin olive oil, Majorcan bread, hanging tomatoes and all the proper trimmings. Here is a list of bars and cafés which offer a full *pa amb oli*; however due to the rapid turnover in the world of nocturnal catering, especially in Palma, some names or menus may have changed.

Palma

Where to eat a *llagosta*

Moka Verd (Sant Miquel, opposite Radio Borne)
Bar Bosch (Plaça Joan Carles I)
Bar Toni (Plaça Sta Eulàri)

Where to eat a *pa amb oli* (evenings)

Santa Catalina area:
Amano Bar (Sant Magí, 70)
Can Mont (Sant Magí, 7)
Sa Llimona Café (Sant Magí 80 and Fábrica, 27
Karma (Sant Magí 62)
Idem Cafè (Sant Magí 15B)
Sa Figa de Moro (Anibal 21)

Centre:
Cafè El Mon (Avda Joan March, 3)
Cafè 1916 (Plaça Espanya)
La Drassana (Plaça Drassana, 8)
La Bóveda (Boteria 3)
Cafè Isla de Palma (Oms, 32)
Gènova:
Restaurants: *Casa Gonzalo, Casa Jacinto, Can Pedro*
Cafès: *Sa Ximbomba, Es Mussol*

Algaida *Ca'l Dimoni* and *S'Hostal d'Algaida* (both on the
    old Manacor Road)
Andratx *Celler Can Renou*
Binissalem *Cafè Can Gras*
Banyalbufar *Cas Batle Negre*
Calvià *Ses Forquetes*
Capdepera *Cafè l'Orient* (Pl. Orient, 4)
Deià *El Barrigón* (Can Xelini)
Fornalutx *Ca n'Antuna, Es Turó* (both on the road out to
    Lluc), *Mirador de Ses Barques* (4km up the road to Lluc)
Montuïri *S'Hostal de Montuïri* (C. Antiga de Manacor,59)
Pollença *Cafè Espanyol*, a.k.a. *Can Moixet* (Plaça Major)
Port de Pollença *Na Ruixa* (Mendez Nuñez, 3)
Porto *Colom Es Pamboliet*
Sineu *Es Baret* (C. Mirador)
Sóller *Bar Espanya* (Plaça Constitució), *Bar Frontera*
    (Carretera Deià)
Port de Sóller *Bar Vicente* a.k.a. *Can Pipeta* (Platja d'en
    Repic
Valldemossa *Bar Romaní* (next to Costa Nord)

Bibliography

La Cooperativa agrícola Sant Bartomeu i l'oli verge de la serra de tramuntana (Plàcid Perez)

El Libro del Aceite y la Aceituna (Lourdes March & Alicia Rios)

La Cocina Mediterranea y el Aceite de Oliva (C.M. Amezúa)

The Mediterranean Diet and Cancer Prevention (Giacosa & Hill, ed.)

The Oxford Book of Food Plants

Guias Alimentarias para la Población Española (SENC)

Teoría i Pràctica del Pa Amb Tomàquet (Leopoldo Pomés)

A Woman's Book of Nature's Beauty Secrets (C. Maxwell Hudson)

Nuestras Costumbres (Lluís Ripoll)

La Cuina dels Ermitans (Miquel de Binifar)

Nutrición y Salud (F. Grande Covian)

El Cultivo del Tomate de Colgar en Mallorca (J. Colom Castañer)

La Alternativa Vegetariana (Vic Sussman)

The Dermis Probe (Idries Shah)

The Penguin Atlas of Medieval History (McEvedy)

The Greek Myths (Robert Graves)

Various articles published in *New Scientist, Diari de Mallorca, Ultima Hora, Fora Vila Verd* (El Dia del Mundo), etc.

Glossary of Catalan words

alfàbia glazed amphora-shaped pot
all garlic
amo caretaker, 'guv'nor'
arbequina variety of olive
arròs brut rice stew
battre to thresh wheat
barral glass storage jar for olives
berenar, berenada snack, breakfast; brunch
blanquet white blood-sausage
blat wheat
bon profit, que aprofiti! = *bon appetit*
botifarró dark blood sausage
brossat cottage cheese
brut dirty; dry sparkling wine
bufador cold subterranean air vent
cafè coffee; café
—*amb llet* white coffee
calamar squid
Can, Ca Na, Cas = *Chez*
camaiot black sausage
capellans 'chaplains', a small hake
caputxetes circular oil-pressing mats
carn i xuia 'lean and fat', Minorcan sausage
carabassat crystallized pumpkin

cava sparkling wine '*à la methòde champenoise*'
celler Majorcan wine-cellar restaurant
cendrosa a 'cindery' windfall olive (see *pansida*)
chorizo Spanish paprika sausage
cirera cherry
ciurons chick peas
coent hot, spicy
coca tart
coca de verdura spinach and onion tart
cocarrois sweet and savoury vegetable pasty
colmado grocery shop
cuina kitchen, cuisine
—*pobre* peasant diet
—*de senyor* lordly diet
cuixot Catalan term for cured ham
denominació d'origen = *appellation contrôlée*
duro five pesetas
embotits sausages, blood puddings, etc.
enfilar; enfilall to string tomatoes; a string of tomatoes
ensaïmada Majorcan sweet spiral bun
envinagrats things pickled in vinegar
escaldums meat in a thick sauce
escalivada roast aubergine and red-pepper salad
esclatasangs highly appreciated wild mushroom
esportins mats for pressing olives
esportinador vat in which olive paste is rehydrated
fava parada bean stew
fonoll fennel
—*marí* samphire
foraster 'outsider'; anything from mainland Spain
formatge cheese
—*maonès* Minorcan cheese
—*tendre* soft cheese

frit fried offal with fennel and potatoes

galleta d'oli (d'Inca) savoury biscuit

gallufa female olive picker

gazpacho Spanish cold tomato soup

gelosía wooden or plasterwork latticed air vent

glosa improvised humorous poem

greixonera earthenware cooking pot

gust taste

jaç flat bed of stone on which olives are crushed

jamón serrano cured ham from the mainland

jipi hippie

llagosta lobster; *pa amb oli* made with a toasted *llonguet*

llevat mare natural leavening

llonguet light coffee-bean shaped bread roll

llova trap for birds

madona farmer's wife; 'missus', 'ma'am'

mancorí inhabitant of Manacor

matances annual pig slaughtering around Martinmas

matancer butcher specializing in *matances*

migas, gachas shepherd's dish of breadcrumbs and pork

nispro loquat (fruit similar to *litchi*)

oli d'oliva verjo virgin olive oil

—*de tafona* ordinary virgin oil

—*de bigues* scalded (not cold pressed) oil

—*de neu* snow oil (traditional remedy)

—*de serp* snake oil (traditional remedy)

—*de Sant Joan, de pericó Hypericum* oil

oliva pansida wrinkled olive

—*verda, sencera* green, whole olive

—*blava, negra* black olive

—*trencada* split olive

olivada conserved black olive paste

olivar olive grove

olivera domesticated olive tree
olivó wild olives (fruit of the *oleaster*)
olla pot, vat
pa bread
—*aixut* stale bread
—*amb fonteta* bread soaked in oil or water
—*mallorquí* Majorcan farmhouse loaf
—*moreno* brown Majorcan loaf
—*de pagès* (as above)
—*de palla* 'straw bread': pre-cooked bread
—*de sopes* thin slices of dry bread (see *sopes*)
pa amb oli bread & oil
—*brut* dirty bread & oil (rubbed with olive)
—*de tafona* bread dipped in freshly-pressed olive oil
pa amb tomàquet Catalan version of *pa amb oli*
panades Easter meat-pies
pan-cuit garlic and bread soup
panet bread roll
pantumaca another spelling for *pa amb tomàquet*
pastera kitchen table incorporating kneading trough
pastilla tablet or lozenge
peninsular from the mainland
pera de Sant Joan small, early pear
peix fish
—*blau* 'blue' fish: sardines, etc
pinyons pine kernels
pla flat; the Majorcan plain
porc pig, pork
—*negre* 'black pig', the authochthonous breed
porcella roast suckling pig
porró a glass carafe dispensing a thin jet of wine
possessió large manor or estate
rebost large larder or pantry

robiol a sweet pastry

rotes olive groves high above the spring-line

Sant Martí St Martin; Martinmas (Nov. 11th)

—*Pancraci St Pancras*, patron of shopkeepers

—*Honorat St Honoré*, patron of bakers

serena the evening dew

serra mountain range

—*de Tramuntana* range forming the north-west coast of Majorca

setrill oil cruet

siquia irrigation channel

sobrassada cured paprika pork sausage

solleric inhabitant of Sóller

sopes Majorcan vegetable broth poured over *pa de sopes*

tafona, tafoner olive press, pressman

tàperes, taperots capers

tèrbol cloudy, unsettled (oil)

tira-tira little by little

tomàquet tomato (in Catalonia)

tomàtiga tomato (on the islands)

—*de penjar* hanging tomato

—*de ramellet* dry-crop hanging tomato

—*de ferro* irrigated hanging tomato

—*de pera* pear tomato (for bottling)

tomatigat bottled tomato sauce

trempó onion, green capsicum and tomato salad

tremuja wooden funnel attached to the *trull*

trinxet bill-hook-shaped pocket knife

trull conical millstone(s) used to crush olives

trullada enough olives to fill the *trull*: about 250 kg

tumbet potato, aubergine and tomato dish

uep! all-purpose exclamation

UIB Universitat de les Illes Balears

varia negra (see *camaiot*)
vinagre vinegar
vinagrer pickler
vi wine
—*negre* red wine
xiringuito food stall, beach-bar, temporary business
xarcuteria delicatessen

Afterword

Since this book was first published in Catalan in 1998 there has been a notable increase in 'bread & oil consciousness' in the Balearics. A left/green local government (2000-2004) decided to support the use of wood-fired ovens and promote local oil; '*Oli de Mallorca*' is now a nationally recognised '*denominació d'origen*'. Despite strict limitations (no olives picked off the ground and a 0.8° maximum acidity), the production has increased enormously, especially on the *pla*. This was almost unthinkable ten years ago, when the first local oils were commercialised and olive trees were more valuable for transplanting to 'instantly age' gardens. Today new olive groves and vineyards are recovering some of the abandoned land in the centre of the island and individual farms are marketing their own wine and virgin oil in designer bottles. A new regulation exempts them from mentioning the degree of acidity. The exclusive Catalan virgin oil Dauro de Aubocassa offers a top-of-the-line Majorcan oil from their Arbequina trees near Manacor. A new, fully automated oil press has opened in Caimari, and the village has begun to hold an annual Oil Fair in November which attracts thousands of visitors. Here you can watch the old *tafona* working and taste the latest oil warm off the press but also cold, as ice cream. Sóller now also celebrates an annual Oil and Honey Fair.

Local wines have evolved tremendously, winning prizes

on the mainland and in Germany. One can now find Syrah, Riesling, Chardonnay and Muscat wines apart from the usual Manto Negro and Merlot. A new *Denominació d'Origen*, '*Serra de Tramuntana*', is being prepared to cover the new wines being produced in the mountain range, especially the recuperated Malvasia (Malmsey) vineyards on the North Coast which won international awards in the early 1900's.

On the negative side, Na Fiola had to close the bakery in Bunyola after the unexpected death of her son Joan; Xisca Soler celebrated her wedding to another woman at Deià's *Bar Es Pa Amb Oliet* before passing it on to a German who ran the place to ruin. *Malgrat Cafè* is now a vegetarian restaurant but its formula of selling only Balearic products has caught on; you can now find such shops in many villages, especially along the 'Gastronomic Route' of *bodegas* and oil presses organised by the local Department of Agriculture. Many of the '*pa amb oli* cafès' that jumped on the bandwagon when this book came out have since jumped onto another, be it a Sushi Bar or cybercafè, but most of the pioneers—*Amano*, *Sa Llimona*, *Can Mont*—still do brisk business. I was contacted by one Majorcan who has opened a successful *pa amb oli* bar in Alicante, shipping the ingredients over twice a week. I sent a proposal to Richard Branson, a regular visitor to my home village, for opening a *pa amb oli* deli in London but it obviously wasn't the right moment.

To toot my own horn, this book was awarded a prize for Outstanding Contribution to Catalan Culture at the *Fira del Pa Amb Tomàquet* (Bread and Tomato Fair) in Santa Coloma de Farners, north-west of Barcelona, despite my rather unkind jabs at '*pa amb tomàquet*'! As for the Pa Amb Oli Band, it still rocks on.

MENORCA

MALLORCA

EIVISSA

FORMENTERA

SÓL

•DEIÀ

VALLDEMOSSA

BUNYO

•BANYALBUFAR

•ESPORLES

SAN

•ESTELLENCS

ANDRATX

GÉNOVA

•CALVIÀ

●PALMA

WHEAT

OLIVES

TOMATOES

SALT

WINE

D.O. BINISSALEM

D.O. PLA i LLEVANT